Creating and Celebrating Classroom Rituals

SiGn & Symbol WORD and song

Amy Florian

ave maria press   Notre Dame, IN

Scripture quotations are from the *Contemporary English Version*, copyright
© American Bible Society, 1991, 1995.

International Standard Book Number: 0-87793-706-0

Cover and text design by Brian C. Conley
Printed and bound in the United States of America.

Library of Congress Cataloging-in-Publication Data

Florian, Amy.
    Sign & symbol, word and song : creating and celebrating classroom
rituals / Amy Florian.
        p. cm.
Includes bibliographical references.
    ISBN 0-87793-706-0
1. Worship (Religious education) 2. Catholic Church--Liturgy--Texts.
3. Ritual. I. Title: Sign and symbol, word and song. II. Title.
    BX1969 .F57 2000
    268'.432--dc21
                            00-011585

Contents

Introduction

I have had the privilege of working in many areas of parish life, from marriage preparation to youth to liturgy to bereavement. I have dealt with catechesis, evangelization, consolation, and celebration. The ages and needs of those with whom I minister have varied tremendously. Yet there is a noticeable constant element in every area and circumstance. That constant is ritual.

Humans are embodied, sensate beings. Though I know my husband loves me, I need to have that love made corporeal through action and symbol, through the rituals of love. I know my friend forgives me, but I need to hear the words and receive the reconciling embrace. I know my grandfather has passed into eternal life with God, but I need the gathered community and the healing rituals of grieving. As Catholic Christians, we know God is ever near and present to us, but we need prayer and ritual to make that presence tangible.

Catholics are a sacramental people, expressing and being continually formed in covenant with God through symbol, action, word, and sacrament. The *Constitution on the Sacred Liturgy* states that our central ritual, the liturgy, is the "source and summit" of Catholic Christian life (#10). It is therefore of utmost importance that we form our children through ritual, preparing them for the full, conscious, active participation to which we all are called (#14).

This formation begins when children participate in the rituals of Catholicism with their families. For effective catechesis, though, that cannot be their only source of formation, especially if their parents do not model dynamic involvement in and understanding of the ritual. The *Directory for Masses with Children* names Catholic schools and religious education programs as having a special role in the liturgical formation of children along

7

with the family. This broad approach to catechesis is vital because, as the document states, spiritual harm can occur if children "repeatedly experience in the church things that are barely comprehensible" (#2).

The classroom is a wonderful arena for building ritual knowledge. Under the guidance of an encouraging and knowledgeable catechist, young people can explore the meaning of actions and symbols, become comfortable with ritual postures and prayers, and gain experience in various liturgical roles. The small group nature of the classroom allows for more intimacy and greater participation, as well as the opportunity to ask questions that lead to fuller understanding.

Yet often catechists do not feel knowledgeable about ritual, and don't know where to begin the task of integrating it into class. It is difficult to adapt the resources for school-wide liturgies or church rituals into those suitable for classroom use, and there are few guides for creating original rituals.

This book answers the need. It is a practical tool for incorporating ritual into classroom activities. The first half of the book teaches basics, defining ritual and exploring its purpose. Several guidelines for effective ritual are presented and the shape of prayer is explained. Various ideas for connecting classroom rituals to both the liturgical year and the catechumenal process are presented. Finally, important ritual components such as symbols and language are discussed in detail. A catechist who masters the concepts of this section is equipped to create original rituals or to modify those already in existence.

The second part of the book is devoted to sample rituals. These rituals can be celebrated as presented or, using the guidelines and ideas in the first part, can easily be modified to fit individual circumstances. The rituals cover celebrations such as the beginning and ending of the catechetical year, birthdays and holidays, and events in the liturgical year. There are also rituals for times of sadness, occasions of commitment and renewal, and other instances in which faith-filled ritual is helpful. Most importantly, there are the rituals to be celebrated every day or every class, helping children and catechists be more constantly aware of God's unceasing presence.

Regardless of liturgical education level or experience, all catechists can use this book to prepare and celebrate effective rituals in the classroom. In doing so, they shape our children's Catholic identity, connecting them to the faith of the community and immersing them in the symbols, gestures, and meaning of ritual life. The children also gain the tools and experience they need to ritualize the important events of their lives, forming their faith for years to come and promoting ongoing growth in their understanding of Catholicism.

I would love to hear from you with comments, questions, or remarks about this book and the rituals it contains. Contact me at Ave Maria Press,

P.O. Box 428, Notre Dame, IN 46556. You may also access my web site at www.amyflorian.com. May God's creative Spirit be with you as you celebrate rituals of faith with the children you teach.

Section One

What Is Ritual?

The way we use and comprehend rituals has changed significantly in the last thirty years, prompted in part by new understandings promulgated by the Second Vatican Council. Thus, many traditional definitions of ritual have been rendered inadequate at best and obsolete at worst.

The *Webster Dictionary* definition of ritual, for instance, is "that pertaining to or consisting of rites." A rite is defined as "a ceremonial or formal solemn act, observance, or procedure in accordance with prescribed rule or custom; a particular system of ceremonial procedure; a liturgy, especially any of the historical forms of the Eucharistic service." This dry, staid, and narrow definition may describe the crowning of the Queen of England, but it is wholly inadequate to describe our ritual life. Our rituals are more pervasive, entwined through every area of our lives. Despite their repetitive nature, they are dynamic and variable. They are often anything but solemn, admitting a wide range of emotional expression. They are nuanced and inherently powerful.

Gerard Pottebaum, in his book *The Rites of People*, offers a much more poetic and inclusive definition. ". . . *Ritual* is the dramatic form through which people in community make tangible in symbol, gesture, word, and song what they have come to believe is the hidden meaning of their experience in relationship with the world, with others, and with their God" (p. 6). Defining what ritual does, Pottebaum says, "Ritual plays a central role in providing us with a sense of embracing the unfolding mystery of life which embraces us." (p. 25). This expansive definition encompasses infinitely more of our ritual experience than Webster.

Further description comes from Vivian Williams:

> . . . all cultures have rituals that identify and form people as members of a particular community. . . . The individual learns the community's rituals and by doing so learns more and more about being a member of the community. . . . Even if someone doesn't "put much into it" the ritual fulfills its purpose, which is to remember or celebrate something about the community and thereby strengthen the community (*Classroom Prayer Basics*, p. 11).

When these definitions are combined with personal experience and whittled down to their essence, the definition and purpose of ritual is summarized as follows: Ritual is the combination of repeated words, repeated actions, and familiar symbols which define, express, and strengthen the identity and/or beliefs of those participating. Ritual defines and expresses who we are, what we believe, to whom we belong, and our relationship with others.

Let's make a quick distinction between ritual and habit. Like ritual, habit involves repetition. However, a habit has no significance beyond itself. When you get up in the morning, you shower and dry yourself off, dress and prepare for work in essentially the same way. Is that a ritual? Despite frequently naming it as ritual, in fact it is not because it has no meaning beyond itself. It is a habit, borne of the most efficient procedures you can develop for getting yourself to work.

Perhaps, however, you teach your children to dry themselves off in a precise way because of the respect it shows for their bodies. You instruct them in a particular method of preparing themselves to go out of the house because it reflects your beliefs concerning their role in the outside world. Then you are in the realm of ritual. Ritual connects us to something larger than ourselves, be that our family, our culture, our country, or our religious denomination. Ritual defines and expresses who we are, what we believe, to whom we belong, and our relationship with others.

Ritual in Our Lives

Child psychologists accentuate the importance of establishing ritual early in the life of a child. Rituals of healing, usually including a name for the wound such as "owie" or "boo-boo" and a ritual action such as a kiss, an ice pack, or a bandage, teach the value of bringing hurts to community and naming them, of gently tending to them and of learning to cope with pain and injury. Rituals at bedtime teach closure to the day, comfort, and the constancy of love. Rituals at dinner demonstrate family roles and become important sources of stability. Rituals of prayer draw children into the belief system of the family and teach them about their relationship to God and to the others in the group. Rituals of leaving for school or work express profound truths about belonging and love, or the absence thereof. Rituals incorporate the child into the family, giving a role, a set of expectations, and an identity.

Once familiar rituals are established, a child can become quite set in them. For example, not just anyone can give the goodnight kiss; it has to be the "ordained" person. Not just any words can be said; they must be the ones that carry meaning for the child. The rituals provide assurance of the known and a measure of control in a world where so much is unknown and out of the child's control. Children who have these needs respected will later learn to accept more variation and adaptability in their rituals, although they continue to rely on the stability of the repetition intrinsic to ritual.

Each family's rituals are distinctive and personal, woven into the fabric of its identity. Children usually are shocked during their first dinner or sleepover away from home when they discover that not everyone does things the way they do. Sometimes they discern values they long for in their own families; often they feel uncomfortable and out of place as a friend's family enacts their unique characteristics.

Indeed, if you desire knowledge about a particular family, observe their rituals—how they greet and treat each other, the dynamics of family dinners, how and for whom they entertain, how and whether they worship, their times of celebration and of sadness. Each family's rituals define who they are, what they believe, to whom they belong, and their relationships both with each other and with the world.

In addition to the rich tapestry of family rituals, we also engage in cultural rituals. If I reach my hand toward you and say, "Hi, I am Amy," your automatic response is to raise your hand, grasp mine, and tell me your name. Think about that for a moment. How do you know when I thrust my hand out that I will not hit you? What then gives you the audacity to reach out and touch a part of my body? In practice, you never stop to consider these questions. You respond as you do because a handshake is our culture's ritual for greeting others. In fact, the very manner in which you enact this ritual, the manner in which you shake my hand, expresses the nature of our relationship, whether it is intimate, friendly, businesslike, or distant.

The ritual of greeting varies by culture, although in our increasingly globalized world the handshake is rapidly becoming the ritual of choice. Still, the traditional Asian greeting is much more austere and distanced, with a polite bow replacing a handshake. In fact, in Asia it has historically been considered an insult to touch another person's body without express permission. In Italy, on the other hand, where a hug or a kiss on the cheek is a common greeting, it is sometimes an insult *not* to touch another person's body. Our greeting rituals define us as members of a particular culture. They tell us who we are, what we believe, to whom we belong, and our relationship with others.

In addition to the broader cultural rituals, we participate in national rituals. If you view a muted video of people speaking in unison while standing at attention with their hands over their hearts, you immediately know they are reciting the Pledge of Allegiance or singing the National Anthem. If you follow this ritual yourself, standing with your hand on your heart while proclaiming these words, you express and define who you are, what you believe, to whom you belong, and your relationship with others. You would not find a citizen of Brazil participating in the same way, because this ritual does not reflect that person's identity or beliefs. Likewise, if you are a United States citizen who refuses to participate, remaining seated with folded arms, your gesture conveys volumes about who you are and what you believe.

As Catholics, we are a sacramental people, experiencing the grace-filled touch of God through human beings and through all things created. We affirm with St. Bonaventure that the fingerprints and footprints of our God are visible everywhere. We most tangibly express this immanent relationship with God in the symbol, gesture, and word of ritual. We mark the milestones of our lives by ritual, we express and define our faith covenant by ritual, we gather and pray with ritual. The Sign of the Cross, the rosary, the sacraments, and the liturgy are all rituals that define and express who we are, what we believe, to whom we belong, and our relationship with others and with God. Ritual, vital to the fabric of our personal and communal identity, pervades all segments of Catholic life.

Sacred vs. Secular?

When I ask Catholics to name sacred rituals, the list invariably consists of baptisms, eucharist, Stations of the Cross, and other sacraments or official rituals of the church. In other words, most people equate "sacred" with "religious." We assume that sacred space exists in the church building, that sacred rituals are presided over by a priest or deacon, that the sacred realm is outside of our homes and everyday activities.

Yet Catholic theologians speak of the "analogical imagination"—the belief that we can best comprehend God through the clues we are given in the created world, in our personal and communal relationships, and in our ordinary lives. The world is not divided into the natural and the supernatural; there is only one world and it is shot through with the supernatural.

The documents of Vatican II confirm this view, teaching that our daily lives are a primary means of encountering God. Our homes are called the "domestic church," and "vocation" refers to our work and family life as well as to ordained and vowed religious. Therefore, we live out the holy not just in the worship space on Sunday but in the classroom, at the office, on the sidewalk, and throughout our commonplace existence. God's presence is just as tangible when I tuck my son into bed with a blessing as when I celebrate an official sacrament.

All of our lives, and hence all of our rituals, are intrinsically holy. Our rituals are also intimately connected, informing and shaping each other. The more deeply my family understands and participates in forgiving each other in our home, the more depth and significance we bring to the sacrament of reconciliation. Celebrating the healing forgiveness of God in the sacrament likewise strengthens us to continue bearing love and reconciliation to each other in our family.

In practice, there is often substantial overlap between the rituals of Catholicism and those of our daily lives. Notice, for instance, the strong liturgical overtones of the birthday ritual. When we celebrate birthdays,

a) we gather the community, those who wish to celebrate the importance of this person in our lives,

b) we light candles to indicate the light this person brings to our world,

c) we sing,

d) we offer gifts involving our time, our talent, and our treasure, and

e) we all share in the one sweet bread that we call cake.

A well-celebrated birthday ritual is thus a helpful tool for catechists wishing to explain eucharist to children, who then bring new understanding to the celebration of birthdays.

In similar fashion, awareness of the sacred in the rituals of our everyday lives enriches and completes the rituals of our faith, and active participation in the rituals of our faith promotes active participation in the rituals of our everyday lives. God longs to pour grace and love upon us at all times and in all areas of our lives. Whether we acknowledge and celebrate that fact in the formal rituals of our gathered faith community or in our family rituals, God touches us and we are holy.

Ritual-Deprived Children

The connections between the rituals of our lives and the rituals of our faith are vital. Unfortunately, catechists increasingly encounter the problem of families possessing no ritual life. Children in these families don't understand Sunday dinner as different or more special than dinners during the week. They don't have healing rituals for when they are hurt. Some don't have anyone singing "Happy Birthday" to them. For too many of these young people, the closest association they have with community and ritual comes from a gang instead of their own family.

How, then, are they to understand faith rituals? If young people don't know Sunday dinner or "Happy Birthday," how do they relate to eucharist? If they have never gathered around the table in love at home, how do they grasp the meaning of gathering around the table in love at liturgy? If they have never been taught to forgive, can they comprehend the sacrament of reconciliation? If they have never experienced the meaning of community at home, can we expect them easily to become part of the faith community?

Ritual-deprived children have no ready source for understanding and participating in the rituals of faith. As their numbers multiply, it is imperative that we connect children with ritual in our classrooms. There we give them a language and an experience of God's love and care, of living in community, of a culture of lived belief. We help children discover meaning and integrate their life experience into faith. We demonstrate that they are part of a larger story, of God's story and salvation history. We connect children to our larger community, a community of faith on whom they can depend in the worst of times and with whom they can rejoice in the best of times. We reinforce the value of celebrating with this community, experientially teaching children the value of full conscious participation in liturgical life.

Guidelines for Effective Ritual

1. The first guideline for ritual is perhaps the simplest: We best lead prayer and ritual with children if we are people of prayer and ritual in our own lives. Your planning of and involvement in rituals is most authentic when it is a natural expression of who you are, what you believe, and how you choose to live. Children detest hypocrisy, and sometimes are more willing than adults to point out inconsistencies between belief and behavior. Yet they are highly trusting and constantly observe you as a model for how to live out their faith. Children need assurance that you pray with them because prayer and ritual are valuable components of your faith life, that you are not merely doing this because the DRE recommended it. Resolve, then, to become a person of daily prayer, participating fully in the rituals of your life and especially the rituals of the church.

2. Make ritual a part of every class if you teach weekly, or of every day if you teach in a Catholic school. The most frequent complaint about this guideline is a lack of time. Many catechists have only an hour or two a week with the children, and feel they have to cover too much material to allow time for ritual.

    I offer two responses: First of all, many rituals are quite brief. I do recommend taking time on occasion for longer rituals of ten, fifteen, or twenty minutes. Yet beginning class with a two to five minute ritual calms the children, creates an atmosphere of prayer and reverence, and draws your students into a faith experience. Second, the time you spend in ritual is teaching. In many cases, it teaches more effectively than anything you could say. Remember that ritual is essential to Catholic identity, and that ritual forms us into members of the community. If we hope to bring children more deeply into the life of faith and the Catholic church, we can't afford *not* to do ritual.

3. Before celebrating a ritual, do as little explanation about its meaning as possible. Symbols and rituals are multi-faceted and complex.

Though repeated, they are ever new because we are different people every time we engage them. At a certain point in one's life a ritual may be tedious, while at another time it is emotional and intense. In a group celebrating the same ritual, each person's experience is distinctive, with the candle's flame, for instance, evoking unique emotions in each one. The goal is to help your students discover the meaning of the symbols and rituals for themselves rather than stripping away the mystery and depth.

This is not to say you cannot prepare them for the ritual. For instance, if you are doing a ritual involving bread, ask them to list all the different kinds of bread they eat (pita, crackers, muffins, cornbread, rolls, tortillas), and talk with them about what it means to share bread with another person. If you are doing a ritual involving candles, ask them to list the different kinds of light in their lives (electric bulbs, candles, sun, fire, lightning, prisms), and talk about the effects of light and darkness. If you are doing a ritual with water, notice different uses of water (bathing, drinking, washing, playing, nourishing plants and animals), and talk about how each one impacts our daily living and our world.

You can also prepare the children by telling them what to expect. This is especially important before beginning a longer ritual. Tell them the general order of the rite, the kinds of things you will be doing and what will be required of them. You can also remind them to be open to each part of the ritual since an aspect of the ritual that seems unnecessary to one person may be the most touching feature for someone else.

With this preparation in hand, celebrate the ritual, inviting full participation by the children. Afterwards, allow time to talk about it. This post-ritual discussion time is called *mystagogy*, which means "the art of examining and interpreting mysteries." Ask the children why they think you celebrated that ritual. Ask what emotions they felt as they celebrated it. Ask about the symbols—how the oil felt or what it was like to stare into the flame. Ask what these symbols might convey about God or faith. Ask whether they have seen similar rituals in the Sunday assembly, at another parish-wide ritual, or elsewhere in their lives. Listen carefully to their answers, accepting their responses and helping them make connections between the ritual, their daily lives, and the faith life of the community.

Feel free to share your own experience, especially as it has evolved over time. For instance, you could tell the story of how your understanding of breaking bread has changed since the first time you encountered it. Answer their questions, but again be cautious of black-and-white explanations. Emphasize that ritual has such complexity and depth that there are few "correct" answers. Rather, the Spirit works in each person. God touches each heart. We are called to be open to new and varied meanings.

Always ask if there was anything the children did not understand. Sometimes that question provides your most insightful catechetical moment, giving you a window into the students' struggles and doubts. Remember that you don't need to provide every answer. If the children "stump" you, invite discussion from everyone. Then either promise to do research and bring the results back to class, or assign the class a research project culminating in a brief report that will be shared.

When you engage in mystagogy, your students will bring to both new and repeated rituals a greater understanding and openness to further discovery. The process by which experience leads to reflection which leads to renewed experience (in theological circles it is called *praxis-theory-praxis*) opens your students to fresh meanings contained in the classroom rituals and symbols. You equip them to reflect upon the rituals and symbols they encounter in the gathered assembly and in their homes. You help them experience for themselves the richness of ritual and symbol, a richness that will continue to be uncovered throughout their lives.

4. When celebrating a ritual, temporarily leave the role of teacher and become the presider or participant. For instance, don't correct or discipline children in the middle of a ritual unless it is absolutely necessary. Rather, wait until afterwards to talk with the offender or if needed, discuss proper behavior with the entire class. If it is imperative to intervene, do so with minimal disruption of the ritual. For instance, issue a brief reminder such as "Karen, we are praying. Please join us." One catechist suggested incorporating the unruly person into the prayer: "We ask blessings for Colin today, even as he struggles to remain focused on prayer," although this approach should be used with caution to avoid embarrassing a sensitive child. At other times, a look or a touch on the shoulder may be all that's needed. If nothing works and the offender is literally ruining the prayer, consider either sending the offender outside the room until the prayer is over or stopping the ritual, disciplining the offender, and beginning the ritual over again. If you choose the latter course, take a few moments with the class to breathe deeply, calm down, and recognize the presence of God in your midst before engaging again in ritual prayer.

5. Get comfortable with ritual postures. It is helpful to observe various presiders during liturgy if you are unfamiliar with these postures. It is

also instructive to do them in front of a mirror so you can see how you look to the children.

- The *orans* position. With arms extended to the sides and hands lifted to the heavens, this is one of our most ancient gestures of prayer. It is reminiscent of Christ on the cross, and there are pictures in the catacombs of early Christians praying in the orans position. It is a vulnerable position, much less "safe" than praying with our hands clasped together. Let it open you to the children and to God as you offer the prayers during rituals.
- The invitation position. When you proclaim an invitation such as "Let us pray," start with upturned hands at your midsection. Then extend them forward from your center to the assembly and continue out to the sides. Convey warmth and openness, inviting the children to prayer with you.
- The Sign of the Cross. We are often so familiar with this sign that we race through it with no sense of what we do. Instead, cross yourself as the Catholic priest and theologian Romano Guardini suggests,

> . . . with a real sign of the cross. Instead of a cramped gesture that gives no notion of its meaning, let us make a large, unhurried sign from forehead to breast, from shoulder to shoulder, consciously feeling how it includes the whole of us, how it consecrates and sanctifies us. It is the holiest of signs. Make a large cross . . . in the name of the triune God (*The Essential Guardini*. Chicago: Liturgical Training Publications, 1997, pg. 160-161).

Note that as a lay presider, you do not make the Sign of the Cross toward the children in blessing as an ordained minister would do. Rather, you join the children as everyone blesses themselves, making the Sign of the Cross on their own bodies.

6. Assign children, as their age allows, to be presiders or co-presiders, readers, candle-bearers, and lectors. The classroom provides multiple opportunities for children to become familiar with liturgical roles. It is also conducive to reinforcing the value of practicing one's role. Lectors, for instance, should receive their readings in advance to allow time for preparation, perhaps rehearsing with you beforehand. Presiders or co-presiders should know the flow of the ritual and practice all prayers aloud ahead of time. Candle-bearers need to know their route as well as when and where to place or light their candles.

   Despite the visibility of liturgical roles, place equal or greater emphasis on the importance of being a fully participating member of the assembly. While it is an honor to serve in a ministerial role, the function of these roles is to enable and encourage the prayer of the people. The most crucial responsibility is actively singing and praying as the assembled people of God.

7. If you are a DRE, head catechist, or school principal, consider developing parish-wide or school-wide rituals. For instance, ensure that every class celebrates birthdays with the same basic ritual. This accomplishes two things: First, there is value in repetition. Children will participate better when they know what to expect. As they grow and participate on different levels, they will discover new and richer meanings. Second, a "standard" ritual extends the level of identification and the unconscious formation of community. When children know this is not simply the way Mrs. Florian's class celebrates birthdays, that it is the way our parish celebrates birthdays, they are connected to the larger assembly. The ritual then expresses who we are as community and what we believe about celebrating the milestones of our lives.

Ritual and Prayer Shape

Every ritual needs to have a clear beginning, middle, and end. Though this seems elementary, it is the rule most frequently broken. People jump into the ritual action without formally beginning it, or they let the ritual trail off without ending it. This creates confusion among those participating, and destroys the integrity of the ritual itself.

Let me illustrate with an example. At an actual parish council meeting, the leader of the council stood up and said,

> I'd like to call everyone to attention. We have a very important night before us, in which we will be making decisions that affect the future of our parish. Before we begin, we need to ask God's help. And so God, we ask you to be with us and guide us. Grant us your wisdom, that we may make good decisions for your people, and grant us strength to stay with our task until its completion. Now, the first order of business is. . . .

This attempt at ritual fell flat because there was no clear demarcation of ritual, no true beginning or end. The prayer essentially became part of the opening announcements.

Although the variations for beginning, middle, and end are infinite, the basic patterns are as follows:

- The beginning of a ritual can be the Sign of the Cross, or an opening dialogue such as "The Lord be with you. And also with you." It can be an invitation to prayer such as "Let us pray." When possible, it includes a song, hymn, or psalm.
- The middle is the most variable. In shorter rituals, it may be a prayer combined with a simple ritual action such as lighting a candle or sprinkling with water. In longer rituals, there may be readings from scripture, more than one ritual action, intercessions, the Lord's Prayer and/or other prayers, communion, songs, homily or reflection, or a sign of peace.
- A ritual can end with an amen or Sign of the Cross. The ending can also include a closing blessing or concluding prayer, a dismissal, or a song.

Prayer itself also has a form. Kathleen Hughes, R.S.C.J., who has taught and written about lay presiding for many years, invented a memorable rhyme for the form of prayer—"You, Who, Do, Through." In practice it works as follows:

- *"You"*—we address God. For example, "Loving God," "God of our longing," "O Creator," "Lord God Almighty," etc.
- *"Who"*—we name something God has done for us. "You forgive us our sins and constantly call us to reconciliation." Or "You created the world in all its beauty." Or "You sent us your only Son to be our Savior."
- *"Do"*—we name that which we desire from God. "Help us who have received your mercy extend that same mercy to those who have wronged us." Or "Give us the strength to pick up our cross and follow you." Or "Heal us in the ways we are most in need of healing."
- *"Through"*—we pray through Jesus, either in a shorter form such as "We ask this through Jesus Christ our Lord. Amen," or in a longer trinitarian form such as "We ask this through Jesus Christ our Lord, who lives and reigns with you and the Holy Spirit, one God forever and ever. Amen."

Using proper ritual and prayer shape, let's revisit that parish council meeting.

This time the leader of the council says,

> I'd like to call everyone to attention as we convene this very important meeting. Please stand as we begin with prayer.
>
> In the name of the Father, and of the Son, and of the Holy Spirit. Amen.
>
> The Lord be with you. (And also with you.)
>
> Let us pray. God of salvation, throughout all of history you have called your people to yourself. You led them out of the land of Egypt and brought them to the promised land. You sent prophets to remind them of the path, and you sent your Son to teach them the fullness of your truth. We ask you tonight to bless this gathering and guide us on the path. Grant us your wisdom and knowledge, that we may be your instruments. By our decisions may we prophetically lead this parish closer to you and bring your reign ever nearer to reality. We ask this through Jesus Christ our Lord, who lives and reigns with you in the unity of the Holy Spirit, one God forever and ever. Amen.
>
> In the name of the Father, and of the Son, and of the Holy Spirit. Amen.

This ritual prayer has an entirely different feel from the previous one, yet it took only a moment longer. If I were leader of the council, I would consider expanding it still further. I would light a candle as a visible reminder of the light of Christ in our midst, or include a rite in which we bless each other with oil or water before undertaking the important business of the council. I may invite intercessions, that as we consider the wider needs of the parish we could also pray personally for each other's needs. I may include a psalm, or invite the council members to pray the Lord's Prayer together. These and other variations can be included at the discretion of the presider.

Important Ritual Components

The Liturgical Year

Including elements of the liturgical year is one of the most conscious and tangible ways we connect children to the larger story of faith. Don't limit this to ensuring the liturgical content of classroom rituals. Immerse your students in the season by decorating the room in the liturgical colors of each season, incorporating them wherever possible. Even if your resources are limited, you can put a piece of fabric (which can be purchased cheaply as a remnant), some felt, or a colored napkin under the candle and the Bible. Your class candle should be in the liturgical color, as should any name tags or decorative touches. The candlelighter, lector, or other participants can wear a ribbon made of the proper color.

With subtle prompting when necessary, children will notice when the environment of the room changes. This gives you a built-in opportunity to talk about the season and the color. As with all mystagogy, it's better to ask the children what feelings a color evokes in them rather than first explaining what the color means. Then you can help them make connections to the liturgical season itself.

These are the colors for the seasons:

> Red—Feasts of Holy Spirit or of martyrs; Pentecost
> White—Christmas and Easter—can also add gold and silver
> Purple and deep blue—Advent
> Pink or rose—third Sunday of Advent
> Deep purple—Lent—can also add gray
> Green—Ordinary Time—Use light greens in spring, bright greens with yellows for summer, and darker greens with brown or rust colors for fall.

Make sure when decorating for the seasons that you follow the liturgical calendar and not the secular one. For instance, secular Christmas begins at Halloween or even earlier, and it ends on Christmas Day. Liturgically, however, we are in Advent's purple, deep blue, and rose until Christmas Eve when our celebration of the Christmas season begins. Consider, then, having an Advent tree decorated with purple ribbons, pink or purple lights, and symbols of Mary and John the Baptist. Slowly build a crèche, but leave the crib empty. During the liturgical Christmas season, change the purples to white, gold, glitter, and tinsel, and place the Christ Child in the manger to celebrate the incarnation of our God.

Likewise, secular Easter begins while we are still in the depths of Lent and ends on Easter Sunday, the very time at which we liturgically begin our joyous fifty-day celebration of Easter. Refrain from the temptation of decorating in bunnies, flowers, and eggs until after Lent is over. Maintain the penitential tone with ashes, deep purple and gray colors, and desert motifs. Then during the Easter season, use all the symbols of spring—butterflies, flowers, baby animals, eggs, water, candles, and new life. Always use the colors and symbols appropriate to the liturgical year rather than that of secular society. Although this is sometimes difficult to accomplish because of its counter-cultural nature, it is an effective and powerful witness to the children.

The Catechumenal Process

Incorporating elements of the catechumenal process is especially profound in parishes with an active catechumenate, where the rites of the RCIA are celebrated at Sunday Eucharist, the catechumens and candidates of the community are initiated at the Easter vigil, and the entire assembly is welcomed into the journey. Even if that is not the case in your parish, celebrating rituals that connect us to the catechumenal process can have a significant impact on children.

For effective incorporation, we must first understand the initiation process. The basics of the catechumenal journey are as follows:

"Inquirers" attend sessions to explore the Catholic faith and discern whether they wish to become fully initiated members. They receive the companionship of a sponsor, a member of the Catholic faith who supports them, learns with them, and answers any questions they may have.

When they decide to commit formally to initiation, they celebrate the Rite of Acceptance. At this time, they are accepted into the community as "catechumens" (if they have never been baptized) or "candidates" (if they have already been baptized either as Catholics or in another Christian faith, but have never been confirmed). In the rite, the priest invites sponsors to sign the senses of the catechumens and candidates, dedicating them to God. They are presented with a bible and sometimes with a cross or crucifix.

From that time on, the catechumens and candidates attend the first part of Sunday liturgy. Since they are not fully initiated members of the community, however, they do not profess the creed, participate in the eucharistic prayer, or come to the table in communion. Instead, they are dismissed before the proclamation of the creed to meet with members of the RCIA team and break open the word just proclaimed. During this period of the catechumenate, they also attend a weekly class session that focuses on different aspects of the Catholic faith, teaching them what they need to know to be committed and involved Catholic Christians.

At the beginning of Lent, catechumens enter the last and most intense stage of their catechumenal process. They are sent to the bishop for the Rite of Election and Enrollment of Names, in which they inscribe their names into the Book of the Elect. From that point forward, they are called "the elect" rather than catechumens. During the first Sundays of Lent, the elect celebrate two minor rites, in which they receive the Lord's Prayer and the Creed from the assembly.

During all of Lent, the elect and candidates are called to examine their lives, especially for things from which they wish to be delivered as they approach initiation. These requests for deliverance are then incorporated into three rites of scrutiny celebrated during liturgy on the third, fourth, and fifth Sundays of Lent respectively. In these rites, the community joins in praying for the elect and candidates, that they be saved from these and from every evil.

The elect attend the celebrations of Holy Thursday and Good Friday (although they are still dismissed before the creed), and they engage in prayer and fasting. Finally, in the midst of the assembly at the Easter Vigil, they are fully initiated into the Catholic church. There is great joy as the community embraces new life in these neophytes. For the first time, they proclaim the creed with us, participate in the eucharistic prayer, and are welcomed to the table.

The weeks of the Easter season are a time of mystagogy, in which the neophytes reflect upon and come to fuller understanding of all that has happened to them. With their sponsors and RCIA team members, they discuss the symbols, sights, feelings, and sounds of the initiation process and the sacraments. Often, they will continue to wear their white robes throughout the Easter season. At Pentecost, they leave their white robes behind and take their place as full members of the Catholic Christian community.

Many elements of this catechumenal journey are easily incorporated into classroom rituals. For instance, when children are preparing to celebrate a sacrament such as first eucharist or reconciliation, or when they are committing themselves to a year of catechetical classes, signing their names in a book with the rest of their classmates is an active witness to their intentions. Even young children understand the power in signing one's name, especially in the presence of others. There is also support in seeing the names of others next to one's own, a witness to the communal nature of all sacraments.

I recommend buying or making a book that is used over a long period of time. Then when children prepare for confirmation, they can look back to see their signature from first reconciliation or first eucharist. This gives a greater sense of history, of being part of a larger story, and also weaves them into the fabric of all the others before and after them who are celebrating sacraments in the midst of this community.

In addition to the signing of names, children preparing for a sacrament can have their parents or catechist sign their senses and dedicate them to God. Although this may be more powerful at a Sunday liturgy in the midst of the assembly, a modified version can be celebrated in the classroom.

Another modification of the catechumenal rites is an examination and acceptance of the Lord's Prayer, the Creed, and other prayers of the faith. Instead of having children merely memorize the prayers and pass a test, there is more impact in exploring the levels of meaning and celebrating them in ritual. This helps children understand the prayers better, taking them more deeply into their hearts and providing a foundation for future use of the prayer.

In the spirit of the scrutinies, children can be encouraged to pray for deliverance, especially during the Lenten season in which we seek to transform our hearts and minds to become more Christ-like. Even the youngest children know of things from which they want to be saved. Young children in my parish have asked for deliverance from such simple things as fear of the dark, or from such universal thorns as an angry temper or jealousy of a sibling. The petitions are kept anonymous, allowing the children to feel safe from taunting. Yet these simple requests touch the hearts of all those participating, letting them know they can bring anything before their loving God.

Symbols

A symbol exists when something interior and spiritual (life, faith, hope) is expressed in something exterior and material. A symbol points beyond itself to something else, yet its own identity is never lost, as it not only points to another reality but also participates in the reality to which it points.

This is a confusing concept, so let's take an example. We are plunged into the waters of baptism to die to sin before we emerge cleansed to enter new life. In our faith, then, water is a symbol of death, of cleansing, and of life. This rings true with our everyday experience. Water is vital, constituting ninety percent of our material bodies. It slakes our thirst and nourishes the parched earth, drenching flora and fauna in life-giving rain. It washes our bodies, clothes, and vehicles, and even provides fun-filled play. Yet water can be wild and uncontrollable, pummeling the earth in torrential storms, cascading down hillsides in mudslides that bury everything in their paths, and drowning streets, homes, and humans in swirling floods. Water can symbolize life, cleansing, and death in our faith, because water actually does give life, cleanse, and cause death. Water is the exterior and material reality which points to and also participates in an interior and spiritual reality.

By contrast, think of a stoplight. The color red on a stoplight means stop. Is it a symbol? No, because there is nothing about redness that participates in "stop." The designers of stoplights could have picked any color at all, arbitrarily assigning it the meaning "stop." In fact, psychologists tell us the human psyche interprets red as anger or energy or explosion, implying that red has more to do with "go" than with "stop"! Because "stop" is not implied by "red" and is not part of the nature of "red," red does not participate in the reality to which it points. It is not a symbol.

Symbols and Sacramentals to Have in the Classroom
- Always have a crucifix present in the classroom.
- Always have an attractive bible in the classroom, preferably on a stand or table decorated with fabric, candles, flowers or other symbols.
- Always have water, and use a transparent vessel to hold it. If you use an opaque bowl, the children will see nothing but the bowl. Instead, use a glass bowl or pitcher so the water is visible. When using it in ritual, pour the water noisily from a pitcher, involving another sense by adding the element of sound. When you bless yourselves or each other with water, do not dip just the tip of your finger in the water. Immerse your entire hand so you can feel the wetness and really experience the symbol.

   This is one time when advance preparation may be necessary. I am all too familiar with what ensues when you give a couple of fifth grade boys a handful of water! Before the ritual, encourage the children to list all the different ways we use water, recognizing that each use requires its own special treatment. For instance, we don't drink the water in which we wash dishes. We expect bath water and play water to get all over us, but not drinking water. Water in ritual is a respected symbol of our faith, and we act with the appropriate dignity, blessing each other or ourselves with respect.

   Even with such preparation, there is bound to be giggling the first couple of times you use water in ritual, or any time you use something in a way unfamiliar to your students. Children always giggle when trying something new; they are not sure how to act and they don't want to appear "uncool." Unless they are a major disruption, let the giggles happen. They will subside on their own, or you can give a brief reminder following the ritual. After using water a couple of times, the children will understand its ritual use and be comfortable with this most familiar symbol.
- Sometimes use oils. The Catholic church uses three types of oil: the oil of the sick (sometimes called oil of the infirm), the oil of the catechumens, and chrism. These are blessed during Holy Week each year by the bishop.

Since only ordained ministers can use the blessed oils, you can't actually use them in the classroom. Bring some of each oil to class, however, or take your class to the church to see them. They should know how the oils look and smell, and the use of each oil.

Although you can't use the blessed oils in the classroom, you can use fragrant olive oil in your rituals or you can add a few drops of vanilla or perfume to ordinary vegetable oil. When making a cross with oil on the students' hands, use enough that they can rub it in and really feel it. They need to sense its healing and soothing nature, smelling the fragrance and letting it soak in.

Prepare your students by reminding them that most of our lotions and ointments are based in oil. Bodybuilders rub themselves with oil to give a healthy, radiant glow. In biblical times, fine oil was considered precious, used to anoint kings and priests or lavished on the most favored guests. Oil is rich and soothing, healing and comforting, pleasing to the senses and luxurious on the skin.

- Always have candles in the room. However, never use electric candles! Though they are less of a fire hazard, you lose the value of the symbol. Like water, fire is a paradox. Candles provide light in the darkness as Christ is our light; in fact, there is always a candle burning in the tabernacle. The paschal candle is the fire that lit the way in the desert, the fire of new life, and the light of the resurrection. Fire brings warmth to comfort us and to cook our food. Yet fire can be fearsome and destructive, angrily consuming everything in its path, leaving nothing but ashes. God's awesome power was illustrated with fire in the Old Testament, in the burning bush, the pillar of fire in the desert, and fire coming down from heaven. Yet these same fires were protective, lighting the way for those chosen by God. In order to capture this rich symbolism you must have a real flame, with the light and the danger. Do not use artificial "flame," a symbol of nothing but sterility.

    Some of the danger is easily contained. Candles can be purchased in attractive glass or plastic holders that prevent wax drippings and provide a small but visible barrier between children and the flame. Taper candles often have a cardboard collar or a cup-like device to catch wax. I recommend eliminating matches by using a "pistol" lighter, available at grocery and hardware stores. There is much less chance of children getting burned, as the flame is a good distance away from the hand. In addition, you can hold the lighter with a small child, allowing even first graders the honor of being the candlelighter for the day.

    If you can, make your own class candle(s) with a candle making kit. If you don't make one, purchase class candles in the season's colors. Make them big enough to stay lit through the entire class if you teach weekly, or to last through a couple weeks of morning rituals if you teach in a parochial school. On occasion, have small votive candles in cups so each student can have a candle.

Carefully check the fire code for your school. Some will allow candles to be lit, but they must be extinguished soon afterward. Some will not allow candles to be stored in the room overnight. (I know of one catechist who takes the class candle home every evening and brings it back every morning!) There is great variation in what is allowed. Read the code yourself and if necessary discuss the issue with your principal or head catechist. Candles are one of the primary ritual symbols of our faith, and every effort must be made to ensure that our children have the opportunity to experience their use in the classroom.

• Use incense. Ask the pastor or pastoral associate for a small supply of incense and a couple of charcoal disks. Let the students feel, see, and touch the granules. For burning the incense, use a small clay pot such as those for plants, or make a bowl out of heavy aluminum foil. Cover the bottom of the container with kitty litter or sand for insulation. Place a charcoal disk on top and light it with the pistol lighter about ten minutes before you want to burn the incense. Place only a couple of granules on the hot coal at first, adding a granule or a few granules if needed. Talk about the sweet fragrance, like the sweetness of our prayers before God, and the wisps of smoke rising like our spirits. Notice how a tiny amount permeates the whole room, just as we are called to fill the world with the presence of God no matter what our size.

• As often as possible, have flowers or plants. Again, always use the real thing! Flowers and plants are symbols of life and seasons, reflecting our souls, our faith, and the nature of people. Some are fragile and delicate, requiring constant care to live and grow. Others are hearty, living through violent storms and the most inhospitable climates. Flowers and plants are finite, and they can be messy and dirty. Parts of a plant die as it grows, enabling the whole plant to thrive. Flowers and plants are beautiful and complex, with intricacy that is only revealed upon close examination. They are always under our feet, just waiting for us to take the time to notice and fully appreciate them. There are so many symbolic connections with live flora. Do not lose the vast scope of this symbol by using plastic or artificial plants.

Child-Appropriate Language

Children engage in classroom rituals more fully when they understand the language of the prayers. Modifying adult language for children is accepted at all levels of the church, with precedent being set in the three eucharistic prayers for children in the sacramentary. (The *Sacramentary* is the official book of prayers that the priest uses for liturgical celebrations.) While staying true to the content of the original prayers, the first Eucharistic Prayer for Children is noted for its simplicity, the second has several acclamations for greater participation, and the third allows the greatest degree of variation for different circumstances and cultures. Our prayers with children, then, should be simple enough for them to understand, allow them to participate, and remain open to adaptations for various circumstances.

Scripture proclamations, too, are more comprehensible when a child-friendly translation is used. The best of these is the *Contemporary English Version*, approved by the U.S. Bishops and found in the *Lectionary for Masses with Children*. For older children, you can read from adult translations such as the *New American Bible* (the translation used in the American lectionary), or the *New Revised Standard Version (NRSV)*. The NRSV, although not approved for use at Mass, is considered to be the most accurate and poetic of the English translations.

There are some limits to adaptations. For instance, even in the Eucharistic Prayers for Children the standard liturgical responses are not changed. In other words, when the presider says, "The Lord be with you," the response is always, "And also with you," even if it would be more natural for children to say "Hey, thanks, and you, too." Insisting on the proper response ensures that our children learn the liturgical language of our faith, and it maintains a tangible connection between classroom rituals and the Sunday eucharistic celebration.

In like manner, we need to teach and use the traditional prayers of our faith such as the Hail Mary and the Lord's Prayer. Many an adult has reached a point of despair, grief, fear, or sorrow when the only prayer they can manage is one of the memorized traditional prayers of Catholicism. In addition, even in settings where many languages are spoken, the entire assembly can bond together in praying a common prayer such as the Our Father. As children learn these prayers, we can celebrate rituals that allow for comprehension and acceptance, helping make them a part of a child's faith repertoire without changing their language.

The final restriction: avoid the dangers of over-simplistic or childish language, reducing our prayers to a kind of religious baby talk. For instance, it would not be appropriate to change "Heavenly God, we hunger for the sustenance of your daily bread" to "Daddy in heaven, our tummies growl for the bread you give us." A better adaptation for children would be "God in heaven, we want the food that you offer, the kind of food that gives us what we need to live a good life every day." The goal is to use language and concepts that are simple enough for young children to understand, yet formal enough for use with older children or adults. The rituals in the second part of this book follow these guidelines, and can be used as models.

Inclusive Language

Since ritual is formative in both conscious and unconscious ways, the words we use are vastly important. For many reasons, much of our ritual language in the past has been heavily masculine. With recent advances in social and psychological sciences, we are awakening to the effect such language can have on girls as they constantly have to determine whether they are included in the images, symbols, prayers, and conversations of our faith. The main thrust for inclusive ritual language is to ensure that the girls you teach are consciously incorporated in prayer and ritual, knowing that they are equally created in the image of God, that their gender has dignity and value, and that they are fully participating members of the Catholic faith. At the same time, boys learn the respect and recognition that is due the female members of the class.

To apply these principles more specifically, let's examine the two subcategories of inclusive language—horizontal and vertical.

Horizontal inclusive language deals with people and our relationships. Proper horizontal inclusive language only uses the word "man" when referring to a male person. When both genders are intended, we say "men and women," "sons and daughters," "brothers and sisters," or we use generic terms such as "persons" or "humanity." This practice eliminates confusion, clearly stating the intended gender.

Many people, when challenged to be explicitly inclusive, protest that for decades everyone said "man" and it was assumed that women were included as well. However, the word "man" has different meanings and implications from those it used to have. This is not surprising, given that the meaning of many words change over time. A disk, for example, used to mean a flat, circular object rather than a data storage unit for a computer. In the fifties, there were songs celebrating the fact that the singer was gay, although at the time "gay" was synonymous with "happy and carefree" rather than a designation of homosexual identity. For these words, though, the new meaning has taken precedence over the old, and there is little if any confusion in their usage.

By contrast, there is ample opportunity for confusion when using the word "man." Even in Church documents, "man" sometimes references all people and sometimes denotes exclusively and only males. How is the reader to know the difference? Biblical translations, too, have often been unnecessarily masculine in nature. For instance, the Greek word *anthropos* has largely been translated into English as "man." Yet in the original Greek, it can mean "man," "person," or "human being." An English-speaking reader does not know whether the term is meant to be inclusive of all humanity or whether it is exclusively male. Rather than putting females in the position of wondering whether or not they are included, we need to be explicit.

Jesus himself sets precedent for including the female gender. Despite their lowly social status at that time, Jesus befriended and empowered, healed and respected women, and counted them among his closest followers. Women learned at his feet and supported his ministry personally and financially. Although the men ran away when Jesus was betrayed, the women remained faithful throughout his passion and death. In every gospel, women were chosen as the first witnesses to the resurrection.

St. Paul, too, listed women as heads of churches and actively included them in his ministry. When Paul wrote letters, he followed the conventions of his day in addressing them to the "brothers," but it would be illogical to assert that he was not also addressing the women of whom he thought so highly.

Translations employing horizontal inclusive language are gaining increasing acceptance from bishops and the Vatican. This is evidenced by the greater inclusivity of the new lectionary, and by the bishops' approval of alternate words, using "people" rather than "men" and "ancestors" rather than "forefathers" both in pastoral documents and in biblical and liturgical translations.

As a catechist, you are teaching both boys and girls. Don't cause the girls to wonder whether they are included in the prayer. Whenever possible, while abiding by the guidelines of your pastor and bishop, be explicitly inclusive. Use "brothers and sisters," "children of God," and "all of humanity" rather than the specifically male versions of those phrases. Include the other half of the human race in your prayer, and let all the children know they are equally precious in God's eyes.

Vertical inclusive language deals with God and our images of God. Employing vertical inclusive language means admitting feminine and nongendered images of God into our prayer along with the masculine. As with horizontal language, our God language has historically been heavily male. Even our translations from Latin prayers have emphasized the masculine, often translating words such as "Deus" (God) or "Dominus" (Lord) into English as "Father."

Yet our mighty, transcendent God is beyond every image, every picture, every symbol that our finite minds can fathom. Any image, including male, female, or nature-based, can only partially reflect God. We need to teach our children that God cannot be confined, that God is as expansive as their imaginations.

I am not proposing that we eliminate male language for God or that we stop praying the Our Father. Deleting the male from our theological vision would be just as great a travesty as eliminating the female. We remain most true to scripture, to tradition, and to our own needs by using male images as well as female and non-gendered images.

This has become an issue in many of our poorer communities ridden with drugs, gangs, and broken families. For many children in these communities, "Father" is the one who abandons you, the drug dealer or the pimp, the one who beats you or members of your family. On the other hand, "Mother" is often the steadfast one whose love is undying. Mother is the one who cries for you and longs to bring you home. Mother is the one you can count on. Although there are exceptions—there are many bad mothers and good fathers—in general these children are more connected to the females of the community than the males.

This has occasionally been used to justify the notion that we should eliminate male references to God and use strictly female or non-gendered language. Eva Marie Lumas, S.S.S., a prominent black theologian, disagrees in the strongest terms. She points out that these children need to know what "Father" can mean. They need a Father God to whom they can turn when their human fathers desert them. Perhaps most of all, they need a positive model to which they can aspire, the knowledge that there is a power at work in the world that can help them turn the tables and become good, loving, devoted fathers themselves.

At the same time, however, the experience of a mother's steadfast love is the closest association these children have with God's love. Therefore, it is most powerful to employ male images that counteract their experience and give them hope, while at the same time using female images that connect with their experience and help them to trust. Both are contained in God. Both are needed, not only for poor children, but also for all of us. Each child can relate to a different aspect of God. Rather than narrowing children's vision to a single image, use a plethora of images and let the Spirit work through them as each child has need.

The Catholic church, while currently debating this issue, shows movement toward more inclusive images of God. John Paul II in his 1988 Apostolic Letter *On the Dignity and Vocation of Women* wrote:

> . . . in different passages of Sacred Scripture (especially in the Old Testament), we find comparisons that attribute to God "masculine" or "feminine" qualities. We find in these passages an indirect confirmation of the truth that both man and woman were created in the image and likeness of God. If there is a likeness between Creator and creatures, it is understood that the Bible would refer to God using expressions that attribute to him both "masculine" and "feminine" qualities.

He went on to say, ". . . 'God is Spirit' (Jn 4:24), and possesses no property typical of the body, neither 'feminine' nor 'masculine.' Thus even 'fatherhood' in God is completely divine and free of the 'masculine' bodily characteristics proper to human fatherhood."

The underlying issue for catechists is that we need another primary image for the Godhead besides the old man, the young man, and the bird. There are so many rich and inspiring images in our faith that have generally been ignored. Yet they resonate with children, helping them know different aspects of a God who is more wonderful than anything they can imagine.

Where do we find such life-giving and inclusive images? As John Paul II suggests, we look first to scripture. Scripture makes liberal use of nature images, envisioning God as fire, wind, whisper, rock, thunder, lightning, and mountain. God is also love, hope, wisdom, strength, truth, and light. God is savior, sanctifier, creator, guide, and advocate. The list could continue at length, each concept containing within itself a truth about God.

In addition to these non-gendered references, scripture uses many female images for God. Genesis says male and female are created in God's image. Isaiah writes of God as a woman nursing her infant from ample breasts overflowing with milk, and also says God is a mother wailing for her lost children. In Hosea, God enfolds children like a mother and lifts them to her cheek. Jesus referred to God as a mother hen longing to gather her chicks under her wings, and in Jesus' parables God is a woman searching for a coin.

In the Catholic tradition, the great mystic Julian of Norwich and the church father St. Anselm proclaimed that God is Mother just as surely as God is Father. Pope John Paul I echoed their sentiments, professing God as Mother.

Broaden all of your God language to the extent that scripture and tradition will allow. For instance, a prayer can begin: "Sustaining God, like a loving mother nursing her infant, you feed us from your own body." In whatever ways you can, include images of God that go beyond only the masculine. Rather than narrow imagery for God, let the language of your prayers and rituals with the children reflect the immensity and wonder of God.

Song

Music is an infectious, easily learned, very effective prayer. In fact, St. Augustine wrote that the one who sings prays twice. In our tradition, music is often used for beginnings and endings of rituals, with psalms and refrains sung throughout. Use song in your rituals whenever possible.

The best songs to use are those the children know without having printed words in front of them. This allows fuller participation, since they don't have to be shuffling papers around and can keep their heads up. Also, making use of the Alleluias, psalm refrains, and songs that are common in your parish increases the connection between your classroom rituals and those of the larger community. In addition to songs the students know, you can teach a simple refrain or two that you will use in rituals throughout the year.

If some of the children are willing and able to do so, let them be song leaders or cantors for the class. Remind the children and model for them that you don't have to have a great voice or any training to sing during liturgies and rituals. Just as everyone participates in singing "Happy Birthday," everyone can participate in ritual song. The church calls us to full, conscious, and active participation at all times, not only if we are musically gifted.

Gesture and Body Language

Incorporate ritual gesture, both for yourself as presider and for the children.

- Use processions to begin your rituals. Younger children don't want to be left out and they appreciate having the entire class process from the classroom door around the back of the room and up to the ritual space. Older children generally prefer having fewer people, such as the candle-bearer, the candle lighter, the lector, and the presider, process through the group. On special occasions or during seasons like Christmas and Easter, the processions can involve ribbons or banners, percussion instruments, or whatever seems appropriate.
- Bowing is a sign of reverence and obedience. When the lector brings the bible to the stand, a bow should precede its placement. Likewise, when scripture is to be read, the lector can bow before picking up the book.
- Before a gospel is read, use the gesture of the triple cross, one on the forehead that Christ be in our minds, one on the lips that we speak God's word, and one on the chest that Christ fill our hearts.
- Have the children stand as proud and united members of God's holy people.
- Have the children kneel, whether in sorrow, in adoration, or for blessings.
- The church encourages the *orans* position, especially for the Lord's Prayer. In many parishes the assembly holds hands to pray the Lord's Prayer, while others practice the *orans* position and still others alternate the two. In your classroom, make sure the children have the experience of doing both.
- When celebrating a blessing, the entire class can extend one or both hands toward the person(s) being blessed. Remember, this is a gentle extension of the arm and hand rather than a stiff salute-like gesture.
- Another ancient gesture for blessings or personal intercession is the laying on of hands. Younger children are often quite comfortable with this gesture, while junior high students spend the entire time blushing,

giggling, or fidgeting. Unfortunately, problems of abuse and fear of inappropriate touch prompt the need for great sensitivity on this issue. If a child is to be blessed by the class, privately ask the child ahead of time whether he or she is comfortable with having classmates put a hand on his or her shoulders or head. If that would cause stress or undue anxiety, invite the class simply to extend their hands in blessing rather than actually touching the student. Another alternative is to invite the class to hold hands in a circle, directing their prayers through the circle to the one being blessed.

As the catechist, when you bless a student always lay your hands on the head or the top of the shoulder, and instruct the children in your class to do likewise. If there are too many children for all of them to lay hands on one who is being blessed, those farther back can lay a hand on the shoulder of the person in front of them rather than directly on the subject of the blessing.

Use your own judgment, but avoid overly cautious behavior. Know that you can always evaluate it afterwards, and modify the ritual in an acceptable way. Whenever possible, though, let the children experience the unifying and healing nature of touch. It is a wonderful embodiment of community, of caring and nurturing, and sometimes the children and young men and women you teach need it most.

Section Two

Rituals for the Classroom

The following rituals and ritual actions are specifically for classroom use. Begin with these, complement them with those published elsewhere, and then create or modify your own rituals, adapting them to fit your particular situation. The best celebrations are geared toward those participating, and you know your students better than anyone.

Involve the children in preparing and evaluating rituals, as well as in filling liturgical roles such as lector, candle bearer or candle lighter, etc. Participation in the creation and execution of rituals is a powerful teaching tool. It also instills in children the value of participation, not only in the rituals of the class but also in the rituals of the universal church.

In choosing and adapting rituals, be conscious of your purpose and theme. Although it is tempting, do not include a prayer or song just because you like it or it is the students' favorite. Instead, ensure that it enhances the meaning and flow of the ritual itself. Be conscious, too, of the temptation to include multiple themes or ideas, despite the appeal of each. Stay focused on one theme or purpose. Experiment and adapt, then try it out. Continue modifying the ritual until it works for you and your class.

Jack Miller, a Jungian psychologist, teaches that people at the beginning and the end of life—children and the dying—can often see things of which the rest of us have lost sight. Children can bring freshness and a perspective that we need to revitalize our own faith. Celebrate ritual with children in a spirit of openness and humility, and they will continually open your eyes to the depth and breadth of God.

Greetings and Dismissals

Create a ritual greeting and dismissal that is used regularly in class.

A bowl of holy water is at the entrance to the classroom. As you give the greeting or the dismissal, the child wets her/his hand and makes the Sign of the Cross, or the catechist signs the child's forehead.

> Catechist: The Lord be with you.
>
> Response: And also with you.

At the end of class, bless them in these or similar words.

> Catechist: May the blessings of God—Creator, Redeemer, and Sanctifier—be with us and remain with us, now and always.
>
> Response: Amen.

Use the same greeting and dismissal all year, or vary it by season. For example, during Easter season greet each child with,

> Catechist: Christ is risen, Alleluia.
>
> Response: He is truly risen, Alleluia.

Dismiss with,

> Catechist: May the risen Lord fill our hearts and lives with joy and peace.
>
> Response: Amen.

During the Christmas season,

Catechist: Christ is born. Merry Christmas.

Response: He is born. Merry Christmas.

Use body posture—sometimes have children kneel for blessing or kneel yourself in front of children that they may bless you. Lay hands on one another or stand in a circle and raise hands toward each other in blessing.

Lighting the Class Candle Before Each Class

The class processes to or simply gathers around a candle, which is on a table covered in the color of the season. Assign a different person each week as the candle lighter. The lighter wears a ribbon, a small stole, or a badge in the season's color. The words of the prayer are changed to reflect the season, events in the parish, or the topic of the class. The order of the ritual is the same, though, so the children become comfortable with it.

If children are assigned as lectors, make sure they practice ahead of time.

Begin with a psalm response or song refrain that is common in your parish.

Catechist: May the light of God's love be in us.

Response: May the light of God's love be in us.

Catechist: Let us pray. God of all goodness, you give us hearts
               that hunger for you. May this candle remind us of your
               presence in our class and draw us ever closer to the
               warmth of your life and the hope of our faith. We ask
               this through Christ our Lord, who lives and reigns with
               you and the Holy Spirit, one God forever and ever.
               Amen.

Child lights the candle.

Optional: Students proclaim one or both of the scripture readings for the day. The catechist may then offer a short reflection applying the reading to the students' lives.

Optional: The catechist may lead the class in offering intercessions, especially if there are disasters or tragedies in the news. The catechist may also invite intercessions from the children.

Then the Catechist extends hand in blessing, or children extend hands toward each other in a circle.

Catechist:	May God bless our hearts and minds as we learn.
All:	In the name of the Father, and of the Son, and of the Holy Spirit. Amen.

End with the same psalm response or song refrain.

Guidelines for Rituals to Begin and End the Catechetical Year

Hopefully the entire parish or school has a ritual for beginning and ending the catechetical year, but it's a good idea to do something in your classroom as well.

Ideally, the beginning and ending rituals connect with each other. The following two rituals, especially appropriate for younger children, give one example in which you track the height of each child, praying that as their bodies grow this year so shall their faith grow.

Another option: If you have space, materials, and motivation, plant a seed the first day or give each child a small philodendron, and tend it all year. Decorate the pot as the year progresses. Notice how the plant needs regular feeding, watering, and care. Plan a particular time during the class for watering the plants, and talk about how our faith needs that same kind of nurturing. Send the plants home with the children in a ritual at the end of the year.

A third idea: In the fall, bring in the autumn leaves and pray about the little deaths we will endure this year as we grow in our faith, deaths that prepare us for new life. In the spring, bring in green leaves and flowers, and pray about the new life and growth that the year has produced.

Beginning the Catechetical Year

Tape a large piece of poster paper, newsprint, or cardboard to the wall. It must be taller than the tallest child in the class.

Before the ritual, invite each child to choose a color in which to write his or her name. (If he is too young, the catechist can write it for him). Give her the crayon or marker of her color to bring with her to the paper when her height is marked.

If possible, have a familiar song on tape that you can play during the marking of heights.

Begin with an Alleluia verse or common song refrain. Gather around the paper.

All:	In the name of the Father, and of the Son, and of the Holy Spirit. Amen.
Catechist:	The Lord be with you.
Response:	And also with you.
Catechist or Student:	We gather as we begin this new year, a year in which we will grow in many different ways. Most of the growth will occur in ways that we cannot measure. We can't measure out 3 grams of kindness, 4 cups of faith, or 6 inches of respect for others but we can measure the growth of our bodies as a sign of our growth toward God.
Catechist:	I invite you each to come forward in turn. I will mark your height on this paper, and you will write your name or initials right under the mark.

Play the taped music as the children come forward one by one. Proceed with the ritual after all heights have been marked and signed.

Catechist:	We want to grow, not just physically but to grow in every way closer to God this year. To do that, we need to do the things God asks of us. We need nourishment from scripture and our studies, we need to forgive and to accept forgiveness, and we need to follow in the path of Jesus. We ask God to help us as we join hands and pray in the words that Jesus gave us.
All:	Our Father . . .
Catechist:	As we begin this new year, deliver us from every evil and grant us peace. In your mercy, keep us free from sin and protect us from needless worry as we wait in joyful hope for the coming of our Savior, Jesus Christ.
All:	For the kingdom, the power, and the glory are yours, now and forever. Amen.
Catechist:	Trusting in God's presence, I invite you to kneel for a blessing.
	Let us pray.

Extend a hand in blessing over the students.

Faithful God, all through history you have guided your people. You helped Abraham, Moses, Miriam, and Judith to grow in faith and understanding until they were able to lead your chosen people. You raised Mary to be the mother of your Son, and Jesus himself grew in wisdom and grace in your sight.

We stand before you as a class today, ready to embark on another year of our faith journey. Bless us as we are, open to your truth and ready to learn more about you. Grant that our faith may grow even as our bodies grow. Let us follow you more closely, that like Abraham and Moses, Judith and Miriam, Mary and Jesus, we may become your living witnesses to the world. We ask this through Christ our Lord.

Response: Amen.

Catechist: Today we have marked your height on this paper. We will leave the paper up for a few days as we make the transition into school time. Then we will roll it up and keep it until the end of the year, when we will see how much each of you has grown.

As we go now to our desks, let's offer each other a sign of peace.

Ending the Catechetical Year

This ritual is meant as a companion for the previous ritual.

Unroll the paper on which you marked heights at the beginning of the year and post it in the same place. Have a ruler next to the paper so you can measure the difference in heights.

Choose a lector to read the psalm, making sure the lector practices ahead of time.

All:	In the name of the Father, and of the Son, and of the Holy Spirit. Amen.
Catechist:	The Lord be with you.
Response:	And also with you.
Catechist or Student:	In this year of our faith journey, we have grown in many different ways. Most of the growth is in things that we cannot measure. We can't measure out 3 grams of kindness, 4 cups of faith, or 6 inches of respect for others. Instead, we have measured our bodies as a symbol of our inward and outward growth.
Catechist:	Rejoicing in God's gifts to us over this past year, let us lift our voices in praise by reciting Psalm 150.
Lector:	Let all the earth praise the Lord!
Response:	Let all the earth praise the Lord!
Lector:	Shout praises to the Lord! Praise God in his temple. Praise God in heaven. Praise our God.

Response:	Let all the earth praise the Lord!
Lector:	God's deeds are wonderful, too marvelous to describe. Praise God with trumpets and all kinds of harps. Praise God with tambourines and dancing, With stringed instruments and woodwinds. Praise God with cymbals, with clashing cymbals.
Response:	Let all the earth praise the Lord!
Lector:	Let every living creature praise the Lord. Shout praises to the Lord!
Response:	Let all the earth praise the Lord!
Catechist:	As we did at the beginning of the year, I invite you each to come forward in turn. I will mark your height on this paper right above your previous height, and we will measure how much you have grown. After I announce the growth for each child, we will all say, "Let all the earth praise the Lord!"

Play the taped music as the children come forward one by one.

For each child, mark the new height, measure the difference and announce in a clear voice:

Catechist:	[Name] has grown # inches!

Then lead the children in the response:

Response:	Let all the earth praise the Lord!
Catechist:	As you can see, we have certainly grown in height. We know that we have also grown in ways we can't so easily see—in faith, in love, in tolerance, and in wisdom. God's Spirit has been with us, guiding and teaching us all year. We have also been gifts to each other. I am proud of the way we have treated each other and helped each other to grow. As a class united in faith, let us join hands and pray in the words that Jesus taught us.
All:	Our Father . . .
Catechist:	As we end this year, God, deliver us from every evil and grant us peace. In your mercy, keep us free from sin and

protect us from needless worry as we wait in joyful hope for the coming of our Savior, Jesus Christ.

All:

For the kingdom, the power, and the glory are yours, now and forever. Amen.

Catechist:

It has been a good year. We thank God for the many ways we have grown. We thank God for each other. As we go now to summer and vacation time, let's offer each other a sign of peace.

Lighting the Advent Wreath

Use liturgical colors in the room, under the bible, on the desk, etc.

Have an Advent wreath clearly visible. The class can make a wreath, or use a circle of evergreen branches with four candles.

In addition, if possible, build a crèche, adding a figure or a couple of figures each week. The children can make the figures out of modeling clay or even paper.

Turn off some of the lights in the room.

Choose one person to light each candle (i.e. the second week you need two people). If building a progressive crèche, also choose students to carry the figures that will be placed that week. Have the class stand around the wreath/creche in a circle, or if it is against the wall stand in front of it. For younger children, the entire class may process to the wreath. For older children, the candle and figure bearers process with the presider. During the procession, everyone sings: "O Come, O Come Emmanuel."

All:	In the name of the Father, and of the Son, and of the Holy Spirit. Amen.
Catechist:	God of new beginnings, you have given us your Son, born into our world as a human child. He is the light of the world, the path we follow, our Savior and friend. Help us make straight the paths of our hearts that Jesus may easily enter in. Help us become messengers that proclaim your presence to the world. May this light [and these figures] remind us to welcome the Christ child again, that we may become more and more like him. We ask this through the One who is to come, Emmanuel, God with us.
All:	Amen.

Bearers light candle(s) in wreath [and place figure(s) in crèche] as class sings another refrain of "O Come, O Come Emmanuel."

Catechist:	Let us continue with our class, now filled with the presence of God's light and life.
Response:	In the name of the Father, and of the Son, and of the Holy Spirit. Amen.

For a longer ritual:

1. Do all of the above, but before the prayer, read Isaiah 40:3-5 or Isaiah 11:1-10. The reader bows to reverence the book both before and after the reading.

2. After lighting the candles and placing the figures, invite intercessions from the children. Then pray the Lord's Prayer together. Continue the ritual with the song and conclusion.

Lighting the Class Candle During Lent

Before Lent, explain to the class that catechumens are now journeying toward full initiation, and they will be baptized at the Easter Vigil. Along with them, we also examine our lives, reject sin, and renew the call of our baptism.

Invite the children to write anonymously on pieces of paper the things from which they wish to be delivered this Lent—selfishness, the temptation to cheat in class, gossiping about people, forgetting to pray, hurting their family members, etc. Make a list of these intentions. They will be used in a modified scrutiny.

During Lent, always have a small container of ashes by your candle.

This scrutiny is written with the catechist reading the invocations. If possible, invite students to read them, having them practice ahead of time.

Begin by singing a lenten psalm response or song refrain common in your parish.

Catechist: May the light of God's love be in us.

Response: May the light of God's love be in us.

Catechist: Loving God, as a mother strives for the good of her children, so you call us toward holiness. Throughout these forty days of Lent, we look at all the ways we turn away from you, and we promise to do better. May these ashes remind us that we are creatures of the earth, formed by you from the ground, yet called by you to heaven. We ask this through Christ our Lord.

All: Amen.

Catechist: I invite you each now to sign your forehead with these ashes as you tell God you are sorry and ask for God's help this Lent.

The children sign their foreheads with ashes, saying in these or similar words:

Children: Loving God, I am sorry for my sins. I ask you to forgive me and to help me change.

For younger children, simplify the phrase to

God, help me follow you.

In this modified scrutiny, use some of the items from the children's list along with some of the following.

Catechist: We now call out loud the attitudes and sins from which we want to be delivered this Lent.

Catechist: From temptation,

Response: O God, deliver us.

Catechist: From being blind and deaf to you,

Response: O God, deliver us.

Catechist: From accidents and sickness,

Response: O God, deliver us.

Catechist: From saying mean things about other people,

Response: O God, deliver us.

Catechist: From selfishness,

Response: O God, deliver us.

Catechist: From lying,

Response: O God, deliver us.

Catechist: From forgetting to appreciate our family members,

Response: O God, deliver us.

Catechist: *(List some of the children's invocations and invite the response.)*

Catechist:	God of the cross and God of the resurrection, you promised salvation to all your people. Change our hearts this Lent. Give us the strength and grace we need to become more loving, more giving, and more faithful. May these ashes and this candle remind us of your presence in our class and draw us ever closer to the warmth of your life and the hope of our faith. We ask this through Christ our Lord, who lives and reigns with you and the Holy Spirit, one God forever and ever.
All:	Amen.

Child lights the candle.

Catechist:	May God bless our hearts and minds as we learn.
All:	In the name of the Father, and of the Son, and of the Holy Spirit. Amen.

End with the same psalm response or song refrain.

Lighting the Class Candle During the Easter Season

This is a wonderful time for a procession with a lighted candle, much like the procession at the Easter Vigil. Feel free to add ribbons, banners, and bells or other percussion instruments. Explain to the children that the catechumens who have been learning about our faith and have engaged in the scrutinies during Lent were baptized and initiated at the Easter Vigil, when we proclaim Christ as the Light of the World and renew our own promises of baptism.

Before celebrating the ritual, teach them the simple sung response of "Thanks be to God."

Select a child to be the candle bearer, or if you have very young children carry it yourself with children walking on each side of you. The bearer and assistants wear a white and gold ribbon, a small white and/or gold stole, or a white badge.

The candle table is covered in white, and has space for the candle as well as a large glass bowl and a pitcher of water.

If possible, have Easter lilies or other white flowers on or around the table. Put a white flower or white ribbons by or behind the crucifix.

You may want to teach the children the American Sign Language sign for "Alleluia" (raise hands with three smaller fingers closed and thumbs up next to the raised index finger; hands circle in opposite directions). They can then use the sign during the singing of the Alleluia.

Begin with the entire class gathered at the back of the room. Hold the candle high to begin the procession.

Done in plain chant:

> Catechist:　　　Christ our Light.
>
> Response:　　　Thanks be to God.

Process halfway to the candle table. Hold the candle high.

> Catechist:　　　Christ our Light.
>
> Response:　　　Thanks be to God.

Process to the table itself. Hold the candle high once more.

> Catechist:　　　Christ our Light.
>
> Response:　　　Thanks be to God.

Place the candle on the table.

> Catechist:　　　God our Creator has blessed us with Jesus, the risen Christ, the light of the world whose fire fills our hearts and shines in all the dark places.
>
> Response:　　　(Sing the Alleluia that your parish uses in the gospel procession. Optional: use the sign for Alleluia.)
>
> Catechist:　　　God also gives us the gift of water. In our world, water fills the trees and plants It feeds the crops that make our food. It washes the earth. We cannot live without water and the life it brings to all of creation.

Pour the water from the pitcher into the bowl. Pour it so everyone can hear the sound.

> Catechist:　　　This water, too, is the water of our baptism. It reminds us that we are God's people, chosen and called by name, called to holiness. I invite each of you to sink your hand into this water, the reminder of our baptism. Then sign yourselves with the Sign of the Cross, the sign of Jesus, the sign of our identity as Catholic Christians.

Model for the children putting your whole hand into the water and blessing yourself with it. Invite the children to come forward to bless themselves.

Catechist:	Let us pray. God of our salvation, with fire and power you led your people out of Egypt to the promised land. With that same power, lead us deeper into our faith. Bless us and make us holy, and grant that in all we do we may glorify your name. We ask this through the risen Christ, our Lord and Savior, who lives with you and the Holy Spirit, one God forever and ever. Amen. Alleluia.

Sing the Alleluia.

All:	In the name of the Father, and of the Son, and of the Holy Spirit. Amen.

For a longer ritual:

After blessing with the water, read Matthew 3:13-17. The reader bows to reverence the book both before and after the reading. Then invite intercessions from the children, and pray the Lord's Prayer together. Optional: Follow the Lord's Prayer with the sign of peace before moving on to the closing prayer.

Optional small ritual:

Easter Season lasts for fifty days, until Pentecost. The Jews marked the days with a grain of barley. Make a calendar with fifty squares and buy some barley. During each class, glue a grain of barley to the days that have passed. This can take place in the context of the above ritual, or can be done as a part of the class period itself.

Enrollment of Names

This ritual is based on the Enrollment of Names and Rite of Election for the catechumenate. The catechumens have their names publicly announced in the community, and sign their names into the Book of the Elect that is presented to the bishop. This is usually done at the beginning of Lent.

The version below is used for children entering sacramental preparation, especially first eucharist and confirmation. It can also be adapted for the beginning of the catechetical year or for any other significant commitment which the children are undertaking.

I recommend creating a common book for names in the parish. It can be as simple as an attractive three-ring binder. When babies are baptized, their parents enter the baptismal names into the book. Each time children sign their names in preparation for first eucharist or confirmation, the page of names is added to the book. In this way, children can look back and find their names, tracing the history of their initiation into the church. It connects them to the larger story of the parish, the universal church, and salvation history. The book can be enshrined at every initiation liturgy, a testimony to the faith of the community.

Choose one child to serve as lector.

Prepare a piece of parchment paper or pastel colored paper on which the children will sign their names. For younger children, use lined paper or draw boxes for their names. Place the paper on a table decorated with the colors of the liturgical season, next to the candle and bible. Attach the paper to a clipboard or stiff material to make it easy for the children to write on it. Place at least two pencils or pens next to the paper.

If desired, have a tape of music ready to play while the children sign their names.

Begin with the entire class at the back of the room.

Process up the center of the room while singing an Alleluia verse or a song refrain that is common in your parish. Gather around the table.

All:	In the name of the Father, and of the Son, and of the Holy Spirit. Amen.
Catechist:	My dear students, today you sign your names as a way of committing yourselves to another stage of your initiation into the Catholic church. This is an important step, one which brings excitement to your family, your parish community, and the whole church. We begin by listening to the word of God, hearing about how deeply God knows and loves us.

The lector bows in front of the book, then opens it and reads Isaiah 43:1-3a, 4a.

Lector:	A reading from the book of the prophet Isaiah. This is what the Lord says. Do not fear, for I have redeemed you; I have called you by name. You are mine. When you pass through the waters, I will be with you; when you walk through fire you shall not be burned, and the flame shall not consume you. For I am the Lord your God, the Holy One of Israel, your savior. You are precious in my sight, and honored, and I love you. The word of the Lord.
Response:	Thanks be to God.
Catechist:	God loves you and has called you by name. You are accepting God's love and care through the church as you prepare to celebrate the sacrament of (first eucharist; confirmation). This step requires serious commitment on your part, and so I ask you:
(For eucharist)	Do you sincerely want to gather with the community around the table in the sacrament of eucharist?
(For confirmation)	Do you sincerely wish to complete your initiation into the Catholic church by celebrating the sacrament of confirmation?
Response:	We do.
Catechist:	Do you listen well to the word of God?
Response:	We do.

Catechist:	Do you try to live as faithful followers of Christ?
Response:	We do.
Catechist:	Do you participate in this community's life of prayer and service?
Response:	We do.
Catechist:	You are making a commitment to this church and this community, which accept you and support you. As a sign of your commitment, I invite you now to sign your names on this paper, which will be placed into the book of sacramental initiation.

The children come forward to the table and sign their names. While they are doing so, sing or hum a song that is common in the parish, or play background music on a tape recorder.

Catechist:	You have written your name as a sign of your commitment to celebrate the sacrament of (eucharist; confirmation). God is always faithful, and you are called to be faithful, too. It is your responsibility to know, love, and serve the Lord more and more with each passing day. Continue to rely on your family, your teachers, and your parish community for the help you need to follow the way of Jesus. Having stated your commitment and sealed it by signing your name, I invite you to kneel for a blessing.

Children kneel and catechist raises hand in blessing.

	God of love and power, you created us, you give us life, you call us by name, and you draw us ever closer to you. Cradle these young people in your arms, and bless them as they prepare for the sacrament of (eucharist; confirmation). May they find joy in the life you have won for us through Jesus Christ our Lord.
Response:	Amen.
Catechist:	I invite you to stand.
	May almighty God bless us all, in the name of the Father, and of the Son, and of the Holy Spirit.

Response: Amen.

The paper on which the students signed their names is added to the parish book. If you do not have a parish book, display the paper in the classroom as a reminder of their commitment to prepare for the sacrament.

Signing of the Senses

This ritual is based on the signing of the senses for the catechumenate. The version below is used at the beginning the catechetical year, and assumes that at least one parent is present (invite parents to join you for the last fifteen minutes of the first class). If parents are not available, the signing may be done by the catechist.

This ritual also includes adaptations for children entering sacramental preparation.

All: In the name of the Father, and of the Son, and of the Holy Spirit. Amen.

Catechist: As we gather today we are beginning a new catechetical year (or beginning preparation for the sacrament of reconciliation or first eucharist). As families in Christian community, we pledge our support and we pray for God's blessings.

Catechist addresses the children.

Catechist: Young people, is it your desire to follow in the way of Jesus?

Children: Yes.

Catechist: Will you do your best to live as a child of God, loving God with all your heart and loving others as God has loved you?

Children: Yes.

Catechist: Will you commit yourself to your lessons this year, that you may learn more about your faith and how to live it out?

(*If for reconciliation, ask, "Will you do your best to offer forgiveness to those who have hurt you as Jesus forgave those who came to him?"*

If for first eucharist, ask, "Will you promise to become what you receive in this sacrament, living out your baptismal call as a member of the Body of Christ?")

Children:	Yes.

Catechist addresses the parents.

Catechist:	Parents, your children are entering a new catechetical year (or preparation for the sacrament of reconciliation or first eucharist). Do you consent to their desire to engage in this process?
Parents:	We do.
Catechist:	Parents, will you support your children in their journey, helping them to learn and grow in their faith?
Parents:	We will.
Catechist:	Recognizing our communal responsibility for raising these children in the faith, will you be examples for all of these children of forgiving love, of faithfulness, and of living out our call as members of the body of Christ?
Parents:	We will.
Catechist:	Joined as one in mind and heart, we sign these children to God.

Catechist invites parents to turn toward their children and sign them as directed.

Receive the Sign of the Cross on your forehead. May your mind be open to the knowledge of your faith.

Receive the Sign of the Cross on your ears. May you hear the voice of God.

Receive the Sign of the Cross on your eyes. May you see with the light of God.

Receive the Sign of the Cross on your lips. May you speak with the wisdom of God.

Receive the Sign of the Cross on your heart. May God fill and expand your heart.

Receive the Sign of the Cross on your shoulders. May you bear the hardships that come with living a life of faith.

Receive the Sign of the Cross on your hands. May you know the healing touch of God's love.

Receive the Sign of the Cross on your feet. May you always walk in the way of Christ.

Catechist invites the parents to raise their hands in blessing over the children.

Catechist: Lord our God, your Son Jesus welcomed young people and blessed them. Look with favor on these, the children of this parish community. Bless them and grant that they may grow into deeper faith and devotion to you. May our example, teaching, and support help bring them to a new and powerful experience of you in their lives. We ask this through Jesus Christ our Lord, who lives and reigns with you and the Holy Spirit, one God forever and ever.

All: Amen.

Catechist: As we close our celebration, let us offer each other a sign of peace.

All Saints' or All Souls' Day

At the beginning of November, send notes to parents. Invite children to bring to class the names and perhaps pictures of people from their extended family who have died. If possible, have votive candles in cups so each child can hold one. If you can't have votives, as least have enough regular candles that one can represent each child. Place the candles around the class candle on a table covered with dark green and brown colors. Prepare charcoal and incense, and place them on the table. Decorate with autumn leaves around the candles.

The ritual is written with the catechist reading the invitation to prayer and the invocations of the litany. If you teach older children, choose students to read those parts. Make sure they practice ahead of time.

Gather the class around the table and do the usual lighting of the class candle.

After lighting the candle,

> Catechist: Today we are remembering in a special way the people who have touched our lives and who have died.

Catechist or a student puts a few granules of incense on the charcoal.

> Catechist: We light this incense and smell its sweetness. We see how it rises up, carrying with it our prayers and our needs. We believe that when we die we shall be carried to heaven and joined with all those who have gone before us. Even now, they stand with us in the community of faith; and so we pray, first naming our biblical ancestors in the faith, then naming some modern-day saints, then naming our personal ancestors. I invite you to respond to each invocation with "Pray for us."

Make sure to include in the list any biblical characters that have been discussed in class. Feel free to omit any names that your class would not recognize, or substitute other names. For younger children, shorten the list. If you are comfortable, chant the names. Be sure to include both men and women.

Catechist: Abraham, Sarah, Isaac, Rachel, and Jacob,

Response: Pray for us.

Catechist: Rebekah, Judah, Leah, and Joseph,

Response: Pray for us.

Catechist: David, Esther, and Solomon,

Response: Pray for us.

Catechist: Miriam, Samuel, Elijah, and Elisha,

Response: Pray for us.

Catechist: Daniel, Isaiah, and Ruth,

Response: Pray for us.

Catechist: Phoebe, Priscilla, Lydia, and Paul,

Response: Pray for us.

Catechist: Mary Magdalene, Peter, Mary, and Elizabeth,

Response: Pray for us.

Catechist: Dorothy Day, Maximilian Kolbe, and Kateri Tekakwitha,

Response: Pray for us.

Catechist   Martin Luther King, Jr., Oscar Romero, and Mother Teresa,

Response: Pray for us.

Catechist: St. (names from one family),

Response: Pray for us.

Catechist: St. (names from another family, etc.),

As each family's names are called, the child places any pictures or names around the class candle and then lights a small candle (with assistance for small children). If they are votive candles, the child holds it. Otherwise, the candle remains on the table.

Continue until the names from each family have been listed.

Catechist: All you holy men and women,

Response: Pray for us.

Catechist: In company with the saints and the angels, we use our hands and voices to say the prayer that Jesus taught us.

Students and catechist stand in the orans position.

Our Father . . . Amen.

Catechist: Dear God, you have joined into one body all those who love and worship you. We thank you that we can be part of this body. Send your consoling spirit to fill the emptiness in those who are grieving the death of a loved one. Hold us in your tender embrace and help us live with the assurance of eternal life. Grant us strength to be like the saints of the Bible and the saints of our day, that some day we may join them and all those we love in heaven. We ask this through Jesus Christ our Lord, who lives and reigns with you and the Holy Spirit, one God forever and ever. Amen.

The candles can stay lit on the table throughout the class, and if desired, a few granules of incense can be added every fifteen or twenty minutes to keep some incense burning constantly. Be careful about burning so much that it distracts the class or causes coughing. At the end of class, children can receive their pictures and blow out their candles.

Dismissal Rite for the Feast of St. Nicholas

The Feast of St. Nicholas is December 6. Nicholas was a bishop (he died in 342 A.D.) who gave gold to the poor and sweet treats to children. Later his name got mixed up with Kristkindl, the Christ child who brought gifts to children. That eventually became Kris Kringle, and then Santa Claus. Thus, Santa is often called "St. Nick." This doesn't prevent us, however, from celebrating St. Nicholas on his own feast day.

Tradition says if you receive a gold coin or sweet treat from St. Nicholas, you must repay the kindness by doing a kind deed for someone else.

In the class closest to St. Nicholas, have a bowl of Hershey's kisses or chocolate "coins" wrapped in gold on the candle table. At the end of class, tell the story of St. Nicholas.

For the dismissal, gather the class around the candle table.

All:	In the name of the Father, and of the Son, and of the Holy Spirit. Amen.
Catechist:	God of laughter and delight, you are happy when we treat each other with kindness. In the spirit of St. Nicholas, we take one of these treats and pledge to spread the sweetness to those whom we meet. Bless our efforts, that your joy may spread through all people. We ask this through Christ our Lord. Amen.

Offer each child a treat, saying:

> Receive this symbol of sweetness. Go spread God's love by doing a kind deed for someone in return.

When all children have received their treat, raise your hands in blessing over them, saying:

Catechist: May our God bless us and keep us as we go to do good deeds. I send you forth in the peace of Christ.

All: In the name of the Father, and of the Son, and of the Holy Spirit. Amen.

The Rosary

Praying the rosary in class with your students, aside from being a valuable prayer experience on its own, yields three important results: First, the children learn a prayer form to which they can return throughout their lives. Second, praying the rosary reinforces their knowledge of the Lord's Prayer, Glory Be to the Father, and Hail Mary. Finally, when you teach the mysteries of the rosary, your students learn the major events of Jesus' and Mary's lives in an easily accessible way.

The rosary is a set of beads divided into five decades. ("Decade" means "ten.") Each decade begins with the Lord's Prayer, continues with ten Hail Marys, and ends with the Glory Be to the Father. Each decade can focus on a particular mystery of our faith. (The Joyful, Sorrowful, and Glorious Mysteries are listed below.) The mysteries, proclaimed in order, proceed from the moment Mary agrees to be the Mother of God, through the life, passion, and resurrection of Jesus, and on to Mary's glorification in heaven.

When praying the entire rosary, it is introduced with the Apostles' Creed, the Lord's Prayer, and three Hail Marys. Many people conclude the rosary with a Marian prayer such as the Memorare or the Hail, Holy Queen, although these are not officially a part of the rosary and are difficult for young children to understand. The two prayers are written below, along with explanations for younger children if you choose to use them.

Catholics especially honor Mary in October and May. During one or both of these months, pray a decade of the rosary after lighting the class candle. Invite children to bring their own rosaries. (A note to parents helps.) Otherwise, string seeds, beans, or plastic baubles together on yarn. You can string just ten together and re-use the one decade, or make a progressive rosary, adding one decade each week.

Before you pray, invite one child to tell a story about someone he or she loves; the rosary that day can be dedicated to the named person. (If you teach weekly or won't pray the rosary often enough for everyone to have a chance, request volunteers or draw names.)

Explain to your students that the rosary is intentionally repetitive prayer. You can pay close attention, meditating on the rosary or the mysteries as you pray, or the prayers can form the background for thinking, praying, or meditating about other things. For many people, it's like listening to music while you are doing something else. The prayers and mysteries of the rosary can act as the canvas behind all you do, the melody that plays as you work, the loving reminder of Mary's intercession and God's presence.

The Joyful Mysteries

The Annunciation—The angel Gabriel asks Mary to be the Mother of God and she agrees.

The Visitation—Mary visits her cousin Elizabeth and they share the joy they find in God.

The Nativity—Jesus is born!

The Presentation—Mary and Joseph dedicate Jesus to God in the temple.

The Finding of the Child Jesus in the Temple—Mary and Joseph lose Jesus for three days, and then find him teaching in the Temple.

The Sorrowful Mysteries

The Agony in the Garden—Jesus prays to gain strength for the suffering and death he will endure.

The Scourging at the Pillar—Following Pilate's orders, soldiers whip Jesus.

The Crowning with Thorns—Soldiers make fun of Jesus by laughing at him, spitting on him, and crowning him with thorn branches.

The Carrying of the Cross—Jesus carries his cross through Jerusalem to Gethsemane.

The Crucifixion—Jesus is nailed to the cross and dies.

The Glorious Mysteries

The Resurrection—God raises Jesus from the dead.

The Ascension—Jesus physically leaves the earth, but promises that the Spirit will come.

The Sending of the Holy Spirit—God's Spirit is sent to fill and guide the church, coming upon Jesus' followers with wind and tongues of fire.

The Assumption of Mary—Mary, who is the example we will follow, is taken to heaven body and soul.

The Crowning of Mary as Queen of Heaven—God gives Mary special glory and dignity.

The Memorare

Remember O Most Gracious Virgin Mary, that never was it known that anyone who fled to your protection, implored your help, or sought your intercession was left unaided. Inspired by this confidence, I fly to you, O Virgin of Virgins, my Mother. To you I come, before you I stand, sinful and sorrowful. O Mother of the Word Incarnate, despise not my petitions, but in your mercy, hear and answer me. Amen.

A Child's Explanation of the Memorare

We ask Mary to remember that she has never turned away from anyone who came to her in prayer. This gives us confidence to come to her as our Mother. We pray to Mary even when we have sinned and when we are sad. We ask Mary as the Mother of God to hear our prayers and answer them.

Hail, Holy Queen

Hail, holy Queen, mother of mercy, our life, our sweetness, and our hope. To you we cry, poor children of Eve. To you we send up our sighs, mourning and weeping in this valley of tears. Turn, then, most gracious advocate, your eyes of mercy toward us. Lead us home at last and show us the blessed fruit of your womb, Jesus; O clement, O loving, O sweet Virgin Mary. Amen.

A Child's Explanation of Hail, Holy Queen

We greet Mary as the mother of mercy who gives sweetness and hope. We are humans sending her our sadness and our fears. We ask her as a friend to hear our prayers and see us with loving and merciful eyes. At the end of our lives, we want Mary to lead us to heaven and to show us Jesus. We tell Mary she is kind, loving, and sweet.

Birthdays

Choose one child to serve as lector. Make sure the lector practices ahead of time.

Either at the beginning or at the end of class:

Set up a table in the front of the room with candles, preferably one for each year. Pour a small amount of perfumed oil into a dish or bowl. You may choose to have donuts, some sweet bread or cake, crackers or animal crackers, being aware of diabetic children or children whose parents prefer they not have sugar.

Process up to the front of the room with the birthday person, singing an Alleluia refrain that's common in your parish. If during Lent, sing a lenten refrain without an Alleluia.

Catechist: [Name of child], the longer you are with us, the more light you bring into our lives. As we light these candles, we recognize the light of your life, and ask Jesus to keep bringing his light to you.

Catechist lights candles, or several children can each light a candle. After candles are lit, the lector goes to the book, bows in front of it, and reads Jeremiah 1:4-8.

Lector: A reading from the book of the prophet Jeremiah. This is what the Lord said to me: I knew you even before you grew in your mother's body. Before you were born, I dedicated you as a prophet to all the people. "Oh Lord God!" I said. "I do not know how to speak of you; I am too young." But the Lord answered me: "Do not say that you are too young. Go wherever I send you and say whatever I tell you. Do not be afraid. I am with you." The word of the Lord.

Response: Thanks be to God.

Catechist asks all children to place a hand on the birthday child. If there are too many children to do so or if the birthday child is uncomfortable with it, the catechist places a hand on the child's head and asks the rest of the class to raise their hands in blessing.

Catechist: [Name] we thank God for your life.

Response: We bless you in the name of Jesus.

Catechist: We thank God for your (sense of humor, math ability, kindness).

Response: We bless you in the name of Jesus.

Catechist: We thank God for your smile.

Response: We bless you in the name of Jesus.

Catechist: We ask God to help you be healthy and strong.

Response: We bless you in the name of Jesus.

Catechist: We pray that you will know Jesus better every day.

Response: We bless you in the name of Jesus.

Catechist: We now anoint you with oil, a sign of your blessedness before God.

Dip your fingers in the oil and make the Sign of the Cross on the child's hands. Then hold the child's hands in yours as you continue the blessing. The rest of the class continues to have their hands raised.

Catechist: God of all creation, you have given us the gift of [name]. We thank you for the years that [name] has had upon your earth, and we ask your continued blessings upon her/him. Let the warm breath of your love fill her/him as you speak in the quiet whispers of her/his heart. Grant that [name] may grow as strong as your holy mountain and as faithful as your Son. We offer all these prayers through Jesus Christ our Lord, who lives and reigns with

you and the Holy Spirit, one God forever and ever.
Amen.

Sing "Happy Birthday."

Catechist: We now share with each other a sweet treat, signifying
              the sweetness of [name]'s life.

Share the treats.

Meditation or
Contemplative Prayer

Meditative and contemplative prayer is deeply ingrained in Catholic tradition. Incorporating rituals of meditation or contemplation in the classroom gives children tools to continue this type of prayer throughout their lives.

The following examples can be used as guides. Shorten them (especially for younger children), lengthen them (especially for older students or after repeating them), or modify them for your particular class.

If possible, dim the lights in the room. Play gentle music quietly in the background. Instruct the children to sit up in their seats with feet flat on the floor and hands in laps, or they can sit cross-legged on the floor with hands in laps. The hands can be turned up, down, or one each way. Read the following narratives slowly, with plenty of pauses.

Catechist: Close your eyes. Take a deep breath, filling your whole body with air. Breathe it out through your mouth. Again, take a deep breath in and breathe it out. Now breathe normally with your mouth closed. Feel the breath coming in and going out. Every time you breathe in, breathe in the Spirit of God. Every time you breathe out, breathe all of your cares and all of your life into God's hands. Surrender everything.

Go to one of the options below.

Option 1:   In your mind's eye, see a beautiful field. It is filled with grass and flowers. The sun is shining and there is a gentle breeze. It is warm, and you can feel the sun on your skin. Perhaps you see some animals or birds in the field. As you look around, you see someone walking toward you. When he gets closer, you see that it is Jesus. His eyes are laughing and gentle, and his loving smile tells you he is delighted to see you. He's coming close to you now. Feel him reach out toward you. Does he take your hand, or does he put his hand on your shoulder? Then he sits down next to you. You feel loved and comfortable in his presence. He invites you to talk to him about anything you want. In your own mind, tell him whatever you want to tell him now. *(pause for a minute)*

Jesus knows exactly how you feel. He understands what you have told him. He loves you. You both stand up and he gives you a hug. You begin to walk away to return to life again. But whenever you look back, you see that he is still there. He will be there for you whenever you need him. He's smiling at you as he waves goodbye for now. You wave back. *(pause)*

Now you are returning to this room. Become aware of the sounds around you. Take a deeper breath and gently open your eyes.

Option 2:   Turn your mind, all your thoughts and all your worries over to God. Breathe it out and surrender it all to God. *(pause)*

Turn your heart over to God, all the people you love, all your feelings, all the hurts and disappointments. Breathe it out and surrender it all to God. *(pause)*

Turn your hands over to God, all that you can do, all that you touch, all that you can accomplish. Breathe it out and surrender it all to God. *(pause)*

Turn your whole body over to God, all that you are, all that you think, all that you feel, all that you do. Breathe it out and surrender it all to God. *(pause)*

Now sit quietly, knowing you are being held totally in the palm of God's loving hand, lifted to God's cheek, and resting in God's peace. *(pause for a few minutes)*

Gradually bring yourself back again to this room. Become aware of the sounds around you. Then take a deeper breath and gently open your eyes.

Option 3: Your body is relaxed, but alert. Pay attention to all the sounds around you everywhere. *(pause)*

Now move inward, leaving those sounds behind. Hear your breath. Notice how your chest and stomach move in and out as you breathe. If you can, hear your own heartbeat. *(pause)*

Now just rest in God's presence, your heart beating with God, your breath breathing with God. When thoughts come into your mind, notice them and let them go. You are with God, and nothing else matters. If you feel your self drifting off to sleep, come back to noticing your breath. Give yourself over to God's care. *(pause for a few minutes)*

Gradually bring yourself back to his room. Notice the sounds around you. Then take a deeper breath. Once more, breathe deeply. Then gently open your eyes.

Allow the children to open their eyes and "return" to the room. Then stand and invite them to the closing prayer.

Catechist: Let us pray. Ever-present God, you are with us just as much in whispers as in thunder. Help us be aware of your presence always, knowing we can trust you with anything and count on you for everything. Grant this through Jesus Christ, our Savior and friend, who lives with you and the Holy Spirit, one God forever and ever. Amen.

Fruits of the Spirit

The fruits of the Spirit are the attitudes, values, and attributes the Spirit generates in those who follow Christ. They are listed by St. Paul in chapter five of the letter to the Galatians: love, joy, peace, patience, kindness, generosity, faithfulness, gentleness, and self-control.

After discussing the fruits of the Spirit, have children draw names of others in the class. They will put the name of that person at the top of a note card, then draw a picture or write the words of a fruit of the Spirit that they have seen that person exhibit at least once. Gather all of the finished note cards in a large bowl. At the beginning of the next class, incorporate the following ritual into the lighting of the class candle.

Choose one child to be lector. Make sure the lector practices ahead of time.

The bowl of notecards is on the table next to the class candle. The lector holding the Bible leads as the class processes from the back of the room singing an Alleluia or song refrain common in the parish. The lector bows before placing the book. Everyone gathers around the table.

All:	In the name of the Father, and of the Son, and of the Holy Spirit. Amen.
Catechist:	May the fruits of God's Spirit shine through us.
All:	May the fruits of God's Spirit shine through us.
Catechist:	God's Spirit is alive, blowing through our lives, enfolding us in God's love, and leading us on to the kingdom. God's word tells us of the Spirit's presence.

The lector bows before the book, then opens it and reads Galatians 5:13, 22-23, 25.

Lector:	A reading from the letter of Paul to the Galatians. My friends, you were chosen to be free. So don't use your freedom as an excuse to do anything you want. Use

it as an opportunity to serve each other with love.
God's Spirit makes us loving, happy, peaceful, patient,
kind, good, faithful, gentle, and self-controlled. There is
no law against behaving in any of these ways.
God's Spirit has given us life, and so we should follow the
Spirit. The word of the Lord.

Response: Thanks be to God.

Catechist: We pause now to recognize the gifts in our midst, the
many ways that the Spirit is alive in our class.

Catechist draws one notecard from the bowl.

Catechist: [Name], we see in you the fruit of [name fruit]. Thank
you for letting your light shine in our class, and may God
help you to grow in love and faith.

Give the notecard to the student to keep. Repeat with each child until all cards are gone. Optional: Only do one card a day, repeating the ritual each day or each class until all cards are gone.

Catechist: Let us pray. Generous God, you give us the fruits of your
own Spirit for the good of all your people. Thank you for
the many ways the members of this class reflect those fruits.
As we place our (or this) card(s) around the candle and
light it in your name, may we be reminded of your Spirit
here present.

One child lights the candle and all place their notecards on the table around the candle. If you follow the option of drawing only one card each time, the child whose card was chosen that day places the card there with the cards of other children whose names have already been chosen.

Catechist: Draw us ever closer to the warmth of your life, the hope
of our faith, and the light of your Spirit. We ask this
through Christ our Lord, who lives and reigns with you
and the Holy Spirit, one God forever and ever.

Response: Amen.

Catechist: May God bless our hearts and minds as we learn.

Response: In the name of the Father, and of the Son, and of the Holy
Spirit. Amen.

Prayer for a Sick Classmate

This ritual is not intended for every time a child is missing from school. On occasion, however, one of your students will be ill for a longer period of time, or will require surgery. Your other students, especially if they are young children, will be anxious about their friend. Be as honest as you can in explaining what is happening with the ill child, including the diagnosis, the treatment, and the likely time of return to school. Then tell the children that you will pray together for the child's healing and for his or her family.

Before the ritual, allow your students time to make cards for the sick child. Place a small box next to the candle table—this is where the children place their cards after they are blessed.

Obtain a picture of the child, either from school records or from the family.

Choose one child to serve as lector, and another to read the invocations of the prayers. Print the invocations on an attractive paper and/or place them in a small binder. Make sure both readers practice ahead of time.

Get a small amount of incense and a charcoal disk from the church. Place it in a bowl lined with sand or kitty litter, and put the bowl next to the class candle and bible on the table. Light the charcoal about ten minutes before the ritual. Place the sick child's picture next to the incense bowl. Give a copy of the invocations to the reader.

When you are ready for the ritual, gather around the table, with the children holding their cards.

All:	In the name of the Father, and of the Son, and of the Holy Spirit. Amen.
Catechist:	God of compassion, we gather today to pray for [name], our classmate who is ill. As we light this candle, may its flame remind us of your love that burns in our hearts always, whether we are healthy or sick. May it also remind us of the light you bring to our lives, and the warmth of your tender embrace.

Light the candle or have a child light it.

Catechist: Let us listen to the word of God.

The lector bows before the bible, then reads Ps 139:7-14.

Lector: A reading from the book of Psalms.
Where could I go to escape from your Spirit or from
your sight? If I were to climb up to the highest heavens,
you would be there. If I were to dig down to the world of
the dead, you would also be there. Suppose I had wings
like the dawning day and flew across the ocean. Even
then your powerful arm would guide and protect me. Or
suppose I said, "I'll hide in the dark until night comes to
cover me over." But you see in the dark because daylight
and dark are all the same to you. You are the one who
put me together inside my mother's body, and I praise
you because of the wonderful way you created me.
The word of the Lord.

Response: Thanks be to God.

Catechist: The words of scripture reassure us that God is with us
always. Even when we think God has left us, even when
we try as hard as we can to run away from God, God is
still with us. In the same way, we know that God is with
[name], with his/her family, and with all of us.

With this trust, let us bring our petitions to God. As we
pray, we light this incense, the pleasing fragrance that
rises before God like our spirits and our needs.

*The reader comes to the table and puts a few grains of incense onto the charcoal, then
stands near the bible to read the invocations.*

Reader: I invite you to respond with "Lord, hear our prayer."

For [name] in this time of sickness, we pray . . .

Response: Lord, hear our prayer.

Reader: For [name]'s family as they take care of her/him, we
pray . . .

Response: Lord, hear our prayer.

Reader: For all of us, who miss [name] and pray for full recovery, we pray . . .

Response: Lord, hear our prayer.

Reader: For all those who are sick, and for the people who care for them, we pray . . .

Response: Lord, hear our prayer.

Catechist: Lord Jesus Christ, you care for each of us as tenderly as a mother cares for her infant. You gather us into your arms, hold us to your cheek, and gently carry us. We commend to your loving care our classmate, [name]. We ask that in whatever way possible [name] may be healed. Help her/him to know the comforting presence of your Spirit, and grant that he/she may soon join us again in class. We ask this through Christ our Lord.

Response: Amen.

Catechist: I invite you now to hold up the cards you have made for [name] so we can ask God to bless them.

            O loving God, these cards are the expression of our care and concern for [name]. Bless them with your healing love, that when they are given to [name] they will bring the peace and warmth of your Spirit. We ask this through Jesus Christ our Lord, who lives and reigns with you and the Holy Spirit, one God forever and ever.

Response: Amen.

The children place their cards in the box. The catechist later ensures that they are delivered to the sick child.

Catechist: These cards will be delivered to [name] along with our love. We will keep the picture of [name] here on our prayer table as long as he/she is sick. Every time we light the candle, we will remember her/him in our prayers. We know that God hears us, and we trust that God will be with her/him and with the family. Now, as we go to our lessons, we close by joining hands and praying in the words that Jesus taught us.

All: Our Father . . . Amen.

All: In the name of the Father, and of the Son, and of the Holy
            Spirit. Amen.

*While the child is missing from class, keep the picture on the prayer table and include
a prayer for her or him every time you light the candle. Update the class regularly on
his or her condition.*

The Death of a Familiar Person

This ritual is intended to commemorate the life of someone the children knew. It could be a teacher or staff member, another student at the school or in the catechetical program, or anyone with whom the children associated. All children, even those who are very young, grieve when someone they love dies. The depth of grief is related to the depth of attachment to the person who died. This ritual should take place a week or two after the death, allowing the children time to discuss their questions and feelings and to prepare to commemorate the person.

Children from six to nine years old often view death as a punishment for having been naughty. If you teach this age group, be sensitive to any questions or comments of this nature so you can reassure them that death is not punishment, either to the one who died or to those left behind. By the time they are ten years old, children are beginning to understand more about the concept of death. Yet children of all ages have many questions about it. Allow opportunities to discuss them.

If they ask about the death itself or about the accident or illness, be accurate and truthful. Especially for younger children, answer the questions simply, letting them ask further questions if they so desire. If a question is beyond the scope of your knowledge, tell them you will find out. Avoid euphemisms like "went to sleep" or "passed away." The children need to know it is expected and correct to say "died" and "dead," recognizing the reality of what has happened. You may also have to emphasize that death is final, a concept with which they often struggle.

When they ask theological questions, encourage discussion. There are no easy answers. Suffering, disease, accidents, and death are an intrinsic part of this world, yet centuries of study and theologizing have not yielded a consistent meaning of suffering. Mainly, reassure the children that although we do not understand, we know with certainty that God is with us through the suffering and grief, and that God's last word is life, not death.

Allow tears, explaining that God gives us tears to help us deal with our grief. (There are chemicals in tears that physiologically relieve stress and promote healing.) Feel free to cry yourself. It is not a sign of strength when one refuses to cry. In fact, Jesus cried when his friend died. It is healthy for children to see trusted adults expressing their grief, and it gives them permission to cry, too.

Be aware that it is common for grieving people to feel angry—at God, at the person who died, at themselves, or at anyone who is happy. They may also be feeling confused, unable to concentrate, afraid, and a whole range of other emotions. This is normal. The healthiest thing to do is to express these emotions, whether by talking about them with another person, by acting them out without hurting anyone or anything (for instance punching a pillow or breaking large sticks), or by creative expression such as writing or other arts.

In the days before the ritual, talk with the children about their memories of the one who died. Keep a list of these memories and stories, later writing them nicely on a colored or decorated piece of paper.

Also invite the children to write a brief letter to the deceased person, saying anything they wish they had said while he or she was alive, or telling how much they miss him or her. Those who prefer could draw or paint a picture, make a small sculpture from clay, or fashion something from construction paper or other materials. These things can be given to the family from those children who desire to do so, but most will want to keep these private things at home. Encourage them to read their letters or show their projects in prayer to the person who died. Those who wish to make more than one item can keep them in a memory box, which can then be brought out whenever the child wants to remember the deceased person.

Get a picture of the person who died, and assign one student to process with it. Assign a lector and possibly two other readers to read the prayers and list of memories, making sure they practice ahead of time. Assign a student to process with the lighted candle. Prepare a bowl with incense and charcoal and place it on the candle table. Light the charcoal about ten minutes before beginning the ritual. If possible, have a bell or chime or other percussion instrument that can be struck to simulate the tolling of a bell. Choose a student to toll the bell.

Procession: When you are ready to begin, gather the class at the door of the room. The candle bearer leads, followed by the class, the picture bearer, the lector carrying the bible, and the presider (catechist).

The bell tolls as the procession follows a path around the room and up to the candle table. When the procession reaches the table, the candle and bible are put into place and the picture is set in front of the candle.

Place a small amount of incense on the charcoal.

Catechist:	Let our prayers rise like incense before you, O Lord, as we gather in memory of [name].
All:	In the name of the Father, and of the Son, and of the Holy Spirit. Amen.
Catechist:	May the Lord be with you.
Response:	And also with you.
Catechist:	We gather today in loving memory of [name], who has died and has entered into everlasting life with Jesus. We feel many emotions—sadness, anger, and confusion for ourselves, as well as joy and hope for [name] and for all who have died. We bring this whole mix of emotions to God today, as we celebrate [name]'s life and place him/her into God's care.
Catechist or Student:	People of faith grieve openly, knowing they can pour out their feelings to our loving God. God understands our pain—Jesus himself cried when his friend died. Whenever we are in pain, whenever we are sad, we can turn to God. We now pray Psalm 23, an ancient psalm of comfort.
Lector:	Our response is: The Lord is my shepherd.
Response:	The Lord is my shepherd.
Lector:	You, Lord, are my shepherd. I will never be in need. You let me rest in fields of green grass. You lead me to streams of peaceful water, and you refresh my life.
Response:	The Lord is my shepherd.
Lector:	You are true to your name. Gently you raise me and heal my weary soul. You lead me by pathways of righteousness and truth. My spirit shall sing the music of your name.
Response:	The Lord is my shepherd.
Lector:	I may walk through valleys as dark as death, but I won't be afraid. You are with me, and your shepherd's rod makes me feel safe. Your kindness and love will always be

with me each day of my life, and I will live forever in your house, Lord.

Response: The Lord is my shepherd.

Catechist: Let us pray. O Lord, you are indeed our shepherd, who knows each of us by name. Help us to know that you are with us. Lift us in your strong arms, hold us close to your heart, and help us heal. We ask this through Christ our Lord.

Response: Amen.

Catechist or Student: When Jesus rose into heaven, he told his disciples that he would always be with them. In a similar way, when someone we love dies, they physically leave us, but they live on in the lessons they taught us, in who we are because they touched our lives, and in our memories.

We have written down some of the stories we remember from when [name] was alive. Sometimes these memories will make us cry; other times they will make us smile. Yet all of them help us remember the precious gift we were given by having [name] as a (teacher, friend, classmate, principal, janitor . . .).

As we lift up these memories to God, I invite you to respond to each one with "We praise you O Lord for the gift of [name]."

Catechist or Student: We remember (one memory of the children), and so we pray . . .

Response: We praise you, O Lord, for the gift of [name].

Catechist or Student: We remember (one memory of the children), and so we pray . . .

Response: We praise you, O Lord, for the gift of [name].

Catechist or Student: We remember (one memory of the children), and so we pray . . .

Response: We praise you, O Lord, for the gift of [name].

Catechist or Student: We remember (one memory of the children), and so we pray . . .

Response: We praise you, O Lord, for the gift of [name].

Continue until all memories have been read.

Catechist: Let us pray. God of all life, you give us everything that is good, and you have graced our lives with [name]. Give her/him peace and joy, satisfying her/his every hunger and need as he/she enters your presence in heaven. Heal all of us who mourn her/his absence, especially her/his family and those who were closest to her/him. Fill the empty places in our hearts with new life, with compassion, tolerance, and love for all your people. Grant us strength to live by your commands, that one day we may join [name] and all the saints in eternal life. We pray all this through Jesus Christ our Lord, who lives and reigns with you and the Holy Spirit, one God forever and ever.

Response: Amen.

Catechist: With faith in our loving God and trust in the promise of eternal life both for [name] and for all of us, we lift our hands and pray in the words that Jesus taught us.

Everyone stands in the orans position.

All: Our Father . . . Amen.

Catechist: In the spirit of God's love and in memory of [name], let us offer a sign of peace to each other.

Accepting the Lord's Prayer

This ritual can be celebrated when the children learn the Our Father, but it can be repeated every year to remind the children again of its importance and meaning. For younger children or those learning the prayer, spend time in the classes before the ritual to examine each section of the Lord's Prayer, helping the children understand more fully the words they pray. For older children already catechized in the prayer, simply celebrate the ritual. A similar ritual can be done for the Creed or for any of the traditional prayers of the church.

Prepare a copy of the Lord's Prayer to distribute to the children. This could be a bookmark, or if money is tight, the prayer could be duplicated in an attractive font on colored paper. Place these copies on a small table with the bible, a lighted candle, and perhaps some flowers.

This ritual is written with the catechist leading the reflection on each section of the Lord's Prayer. If you teach older children, however, involve them in leading the different reflections, ensuring that they read and practice beforehand.

As the class processes into the room and gathers around the table, sing a psalm response or Alleluia refrain that is common in your parish.

Catechist:	We have been studying and examining the prayer that Jesus taught us. Now we gather to once again accept it as our own prayer. In the name of the Father, and of the Son, and of the Holy Spirit.
Response:	Amen.
Catechist:	We have a loving parent, who knew us before we were born, who knows us better than we know ourselves, who loves us with all of our weaknesses and strengths, all of our successes and failures.
	And so we pray: Our Father.

Response:	Our Father.
Catechist:	God is always and everywhere, throughout the earth and in the depths of our souls. Wherever God dwells is heaven.
	And so we pray: Who art in heaven.
Response:	Who art in heaven.
Catechist:	God is deserving of all our praise and thanksgiving. The oceans and rivers, the flowers and plants, the skies and clouds, the animals and fish, the earth and all it holds rejoice in God. Created in God's image, we especially honor the One who gives us life.
	And so we pray: Hallowed be thy name.
Response:	Hallowed be thy name.
Catechist:	In God's reign there is peace—not fighting, weapons, murders, drugs, and war. In God's reign there is respect for each person—not prejudice, teasing, hatred, and intolerance. In God's reign, there is justice—not poverty, torture, and unfair systems. We long for such a world.
	And so we pray: Thy kingdom come.
Response:	Thy kingdom come.
Catechist:	The angels and the saints rejoice in the presence of God and delight in doing God's will. If we want to bring about God's reign on earth, we must follow their example. God's will is always for the good, always for love, always for growth, always for peace.
	And so we pray: Thy will be done on earth as it is in heaven.
Response:	Thy will be done on earth as it is in heaven.
Catechist:	Everything we have is a gift from God. We don't always get everything we want, but God will give us everything we need. Each day we commit ourselves anew, looking to God for our emotional, physical, and spiritual food, trusting in God's abundant love.
	And so we pray: Give us this day our daily bread.

Response:	Give us this day our daily bread.
Catechist:	There is no sin so big that God will not forgive us when we are sorry. God will always take us back and love us. Yet it's so hard to forgive other people when they hurt us. We get angry. We want to hurt them as they hurt us. We hold a grudge and refuse to let them back into our hearts. That is not what God wants, and if we are honest, it's not really what we want, either. We want the strength to act like God.

And so we pray: Forgive us our trespasses as we forgive those who trespass against us. |
| Response: | Forgive us our trespasses as we forgive those who trespass against us. |
| Catechist: | Opportunities for sin are everywhere, but so are opportunities for grace. It is our choice. We decide, no matter what situations we find ourselves in. We need courage to resist, especially when the temptations seem so cool, or it seems that everyone else is doing it. We need God's help.

And so we pray: Lead us not into temptation, but deliver us from evil. |
| Response: | Lead us not into temptation, but deliver us from evil. |
| Catechist: | All praise, honor, and glory belong to God.

And so we pray: For thine is the kingdom and the power and the glory, now and forever. |
| Response: | For thine is the kingdom and the power and the glory, now and forever. |
| Catechist: | We accept this prayer from the mouth of Jesus. We make it our own.

And so we pray: Amen. |
| Response: | Amen. |
| Catechist: | Receive now the Lord's Prayer to which you have given your consent. Each time you pray it, may you know the presence of God in your heart and live ever more the presence of God in your life. |

Distribute the copies of the Lord's Prayer to each child. Then invite the children to kneel for a blessing.

Catechist: Gracious God, as a father loves his children, protecting and raising them, so you care for these students. Let the words of this prayer, uttered by your Son, steady them like a rock, forming their lives and bringing them ever closer to you.

May Almighty God bless all of us, in the name of the Father and of the Son and of the Holy Spirit.

Response: Amen.

End with an Alleluia verse.

Accepting the Hail Mary

This ritual can be celebrated when the children learn the Hail Mary, but it can be repeated every year to remind the children again of its importance and meaning. For younger children or those learning the prayer, spend time in the classes before the ritual to examine each section of the Hail Mary, helping the children understand more fully the words they pray. For older children already catechized in the prayer, simply celebrate the ritual. A similar ritual can be done for any of the traditional prayers of the church.

Prepare a copy of the Hail Mary to distribute to the children. This could be a bookmark, or if money is tight, the prayer could be duplicated in an attractive font on colored paper. Place these copies on a small table with the bible, a lighted candle, and perhaps some flowers.

This ritual is written with the catechist leading the reflection on each section of the Hail Mary. If you teach older children, however, involve them in leading the different reflections, ensuring that they read and practice beforehand.

As the class processes into the room and gathers around the table, sing a psalm response or Alleluia refrain that is common in your parish.

Catechist: We have been studying the prayer formed from the words of the angel and inspired by Mary's acceptance of God's word. Now we gather to accept it once again as our own prayer.

In the name of the Father, and of the Son, and of the Holy Spirit.

Response: Amen.

Catechist: We greet Mary in the angel's words, knowing that God's spirit fills her heart with the same grace and blessings that God longs to give to us.

And so we pray: Hail Mary, full of grace.

Response:	Hail Mary, full of grace.
Catechist:	The Lord is with each one of us always. With the same phrase we hear when we gather together at Mass, we pray: The Lord is with you.
Response:	The Lord is with you.
Catechist:	God is the source of all life, and God has blessed women with the ability to bring life into the world through their bodies. Mary agreed to give life to God on the earth when it was risky to do so. She didn't know what the future would hold. She had to trust only in God's word to her. Because she trusted, because she believed, because she said yes, God blessed her.

And so we pray: Blessed are you among women. |
| Response: | Blessed are you among women. |
| Catechist: | The fruit of Mary's womb, the life that Mary brought forth into the world, is God's own child, given so that all of us might live. Jesus is our Savior, our Redeemer, our Lord.

And so we pray: Blessed is the fruit of your womb, Jesus. |
| Response: | Blessed is the fruit of your womb, Jesus. |
| Catechist: | Mary is holy as we try to be holy, and Mary knows what it means to bring God into the world. We don't need to have a baby physically in order to do the same thing. We bring God to the world in many ways, especially by living the commandments and loving one another. We, too, can be like Mary and give birth to God.

And so we pray: Holy Mary, Mother of God. |
| Response: | Holy Mary, Mother of God. |
| Catechist: | It is not easy to live a good Christian life, to be honest, kind, prayerful, and loving. We make mistakes, and we sin against God and against each other. We need forgiveness and we need prayers every day to keep from sinning again. |

And so we pray: Pray for us sinners now.

Response: Pray for us sinners now.

Catechist: Mary was there when Jesus died. After he came down
                 from the cross she held his body in her loving arms. We
                 believe that when we die, we will leave our life on earth
                 and enter new life in heaven. We want Mary and the
                 saints to be with us on that journey, guiding us, holding
                 us, and giving us strength.

                 And so we pray: And at the hour of our death.

Response: And at the hour of our death.

Catechist: We accept this prayer from Mary and the angel. We
                 make it our own.

                 And so we pray: Amen.

Response: Amen.

Catechist: Receive now the Hail Mary to which you have given
                 your consent. Each time you pray it, may you know the
                 presence of the mother of God. Know her also as your
                 own mother in the Spirit, holding you in her heart and
                 helping you to live as she did.

*Distribute the copies of the Hail Mary to each child. Then invite the children to kneel
for a blessing.*

Catechist: Gracious God, you called Mary through the words of an
                 angel, and her "yes" to you allowed Jesus to be born
                 into the world. You call each of us through the angels in
                 our lives, asking us also to follow your will. You give us
                 Mary as our spiritual mother to guide us on the journey.
                 Let the words of this prayer, uttered by the angel and
                 formed by Mary's life, open our ears to your word and
                 open our hearts to your will, that in all things we may
                 grow closer to you in love. May Almighty God bless all
                 of us, in the name of the Father and of the Son and of
                 the Holy Spirit.

Response: Amen.

End with an Alleluia verse.

Accepting the Apostles' Creed

The Apostles' Creed is an ancient prayer used at baptisms in the early Roman church. It is called the Apostles' Creed because it is believed to summarize the teachings of the apostles. The Nicene Creed, which we profess during the Mass, was written at the Council of Nicea in 325. The purpose of the Nicene Creed was to summarize and clarify the beliefs of the church in such a way as to refute the Arians, who declared that Jesus was simply a creature of God, but not God himself. (That is why it includes the litany of phrases: "God from God, Light from Light, true God from true God, begotten not made. . . .") The two creeds complement each other; both are important in Catholic life.

This ritual can be celebrated when the children learn the Apostles' Creed, but it can be repeated every year to remind the children again of its importance and meaning. For younger children or those learning the prayer, spend time in the classes before the ritual to examine each section of the Creed, helping the children understand more fully the words they pray. For older children already catechized in the prayer, simply celebrate the ritual. A similar ritual can be done for any of the traditional prayers of the church.

Prepare a copy of the Apostles' Creed to distribute to the children. This could be a bookmark, or if money is tight, the prayer could be duplicated in an attractive font on colored paper. Place these copies on a small table with the bible, a lighted candle, and perhaps some flowers.

This ritual is written with the catechist leading the reflection on each section of the Creed. If you teach older children, however, involve them in leading the different reflections, ensuring that they read and practice beforehand.

Procession: As the class processes into the room and gathers around the table, sing a psalm response or Alleluia refrain that is common in your parish.

Catechist:	We have been studying and examining the prayer of our faith, the faith handed down to us from the apostles who lived and prayed with Jesus. Now we gather to accept it once again as our own prayer.

In the name of the Father, and of the Son, and of the Holy Spirit.

Response: Amen.

Catechist: Jesus taught us that we can call God our Father. This same God that we dare to address as a parent is the God who created the universe, the stars, the sun, the moon and the planets. This is the God who gave birth to the whole world, all the insects and animals, the clouds and the lightning, the trees and flowers. This is the God who created human beings; each one of us special, precious, and unique.

               And so we pray: I believe in God, the Father Almighty, Creator of heaven and earth.

Response: I believe in God, the Father Almighty, Creator of heaven and earth.

Catechist: God's love, which is greater than anything we can imagine, physically entered our world when Jesus became human. Jesus is our friend and brother, yet Jesus is the Son of God, our Savior. We choose to follow Jesus as our Lord and live as he did.

               And so we pray: I believe in Jesus Christ, his only Son, our Lord.

Response: I believe in Jesus Christ, his only Son, our Lord.

Catechist: Two things were necessary for Jesus to come to us. First, God's Spirit made it possible for Jesus to be born as a human and still be God. Second, Mary's "yes" to the angel meant she agreed to be the mother of God's own Son. Because we know the Spirit acts in us, too, we know that we can join Mary in saying yes to God's life in our world.

               And so we pray: He was conceived by the power of the Holy Spirit and born of the Virgin Mary.

Response: He was conceived by the power of the Holy Spirit and born of the Virgin Mary.

Catechist: Sometimes we get hurt. It can be a physical hurt—when we fall off a bike, burn our tongues on hot food, or slam a finger in a door. It can be a heart hurt—when someone yells at us, says mean things to us, or teases us, or when someone we love is sick. Jesus suffered, too. He was turned over to a Roman judge when he had done nothing wrong. His best friends ran away when he needed them the most. The guards made fun of him, spit on him, and whipped him. Jesus understands every hurt we could ever have.

And so we pray: He suffered under Pontius Pilate.

Response: He suffered under Pontius Pilate.

Catechist: Jesus gave everything out of love for us. He did not lie to get out of it. He did not try to blame someone else. He did not shout at people or get revenge because of what they were doing to him. He stayed true to God's law. He forgave those who hurt him. He was nailed to a cross and died in pain. His friends thought all their dreams of God's reign were gone because Jesus was dead. One kind and faithful friend took his body down from the cross and buried him in a new grave.

And so we pray: Was crucified, died, and was buried.

Response: Was crucified, died, and was buried.

Catechist: Jesus really did die; he descended into the place of the dead. When he did so, he brought hope and salvation even to those who had rejected God. He conquered death and the power of evil. Jesus brings life to us, too, no matter how far away from God we may be.

And so we pray: He descended into hell.

Response: He descended into hell.

Catechist: The dreams of God's reign were not ended as the disciples feared. On the third day after Jesus died, God raised him from the dead. Jesus appeared first to Mary Magdalene, then to all the apostles. By raising Jesus from the dead, God showed us that evil and death are not the final word. The power of love, the power of life, the power of God, are greater than anything else. No matter what happens in our lives, we trust that God will work to bring something better out of it.

And so we pray: On the third day, he rose again.

Response: On the third day, he rose again.

Catechist: Jesus led the way for us, rising to heaven to be with God. Jesus is at God's right hand, working with and through us to bring the reign of God to the earth. Before he left, Jesus promised to prepare a place for us in heaven, too, that when we die we may join God, the angels, and all the saints in everlasting joy.

And so we pray: He ascended into heaven, and is seated at the right hand of the Father.

Response: He ascended into heaven, and is seated at the right hand of the Father.

Catechist: Jesus told his disciples that even though his body was gone, he would be with us forever. He gave us the responsibility to be his witnesses, to be his hands, his feet, and his mouth on earth. We are the body of Christ. Jesus doesn't make us do anything, though. God created us with free will, which means that we choose how we are going to act. We can do true and loving things, or we can do mean and dishonest things. We can decide to follow Jesus, or we can decide not to. When we die, Jesus will look at our lives with us to see how well we obeyed God's commands.

And so we pray: He will come again to judge the living and the dead.

Response: He will come again to judge the living and the dead.

Catechist: The Holy Spirit is God living in us. The Spirit keeps teaching us what we need to know about God. The Spirit gives us everything we need to do God's will. The Spirit is in our hearts and minds, helping us to choose what is right. The Spirit is with us even when we are scared, sad, crying, or alone. We have the strength and the wisdom to follow Jesus because we have been given the power of the Spirit.

And so we pray: I believe in the Holy Spirit.

Response: I believe in the Holy Spirit.

Catechist: "Catholic" means "universal," because Jesus told us to bring the good news to the ends of the earth. We believe in the church and listen to its teachings, because Christ, through the Spirit, makes the church holy and leads it in the truth. We know the church is guided by God to bring us to greater holiness. As members of the church, we gather together to pray and worship God every week. This is our faith family, our community in Christ.

And so we pray: The holy catholic church.

Response: The holy catholic church.

Catechist: All humans share in God. All of us are connected to each other, whether living or dead. St. Paul used the word "saints" to describe everyone who follows Christ and accepts God's teachings. We are the living saints. Those who have died and are in heaven are the saints from the past. Some people are officially recognized as saints by the Catholic church, but there are countless more saints who live and die in Christ. We join in prayer and faith, both with those who have lived and died before us, and with those living now. We are a community in God.

And so we pray: The communion of saints.

Response: The communion of saints.

Catechist: There is no sin too big for God to forgive. When we sin, God comes to find us like the woman searching for a lost coin or the shepherd searching for a lost sheep. Whenever we repent, whenever we are sorry, whenever we come before God and the community to ask for forgiveness, God will take us back and hold us gently in divine arms. God will give us new life and new strength to keep from sinning again. God will also help us forgive other people with the same love and care with which we have been forgiven. True love forgives and accepts forgiveness.

And so we pray: The forgiveness of sins.

Response: The forgiveness of sins.

Catechist: When we die, our physical body remains in the earth while our souls go to heaven. One day, our bodies will also be raised. They will be glorified and join again with our souls in heaven.

And so we pray: The resurrection of the body.

Response: The resurrection of the body.

Catechist: Everything in this life has an end, but Jesus promises us
              eternal life. When we die and join with God, the angels,
              and all the saints in heaven, our joy will never go away.
              We can't understand exactly what that will be like. We
              do know that it will be wonderful, all tears will be
              wiped away, there will be no more death or sadness,
              and we will be at peace. We believe in this promise.

              And so we pray: And life everlasting.

Response: And life everlasting.

Catechist: This is the faith of our church, and we are proud to
              profess it. We claim it as our own. We hold it always in
              our hearts.

              And so we pray: Amen.

Response: Amen.

Catechist: Receive now the Apostles' Creed to which you have
              given your consent. Each time you pray it, may it remind
              you of the wonderful tradition of faith that has been
              passed down from generation to generation.

Distribute the copies of the Apostles' Creed to each child. Then invite the children to kneel for a blessing.

Catechist: God of history, you created us in love. In love you sent
              Jesus to be our Savior, and in love you remain with us
              always through the Holy Spirit. We believe in you, and
              we believe all that Jesus taught us. Help us to live out our
              faith every day, the same faith carried down to us from
              the apostles. Like them, may we be witnesses of your
              love and truth to everyone. May we grow ever closer to
              your own wonderful light, and may Almighty God bless
              all of us, in the name of the Father and of the Son and of
              the Holy Spirit.

Response: Amen.

End with an Alleluia verse.

St. Valentine's Day

We don't know much about St. Valentine with certainty. There are actually three Valentines listed in the martyrologies of the early church. The most common belief is that Valentine, a bishop near Rome, was thrown in jail for defying the law and performing marriages. While in jail, he fell in love with his jailer's blind daughter and restored her sight. Just before he died, he wrote her a letter that he signed, "Your Valentine." Because of this he has become the patron saint of love. Sending and receiving Valentines mark his feast day of February 14.

Earlier in the week, instruct the students to bring a Valentine card or treat for each member of the class. These can be purchased at a store, or they can be homemade. They can be signed by the givers if they so choose.

Select one child to be lector, allowing time to practice beforehand.

On St. Valentine's Day, place a box or bag with each child's name on it on the counter or on the floor. As they enter the classroom, students distribute cards and treats into the appropriate box or bag.

When the class is assembled and you are ready to begin the ritual, gather the students at the door of the classroom and hand each of them the box or bag for a different student.

Process from the door of the classroom around the back of the room and up to the candle table. Sing an Alleluia verse or a song about loving one another.

When you reach the candle table, have the children gather around it in a circle, holding their boxes or bags.

> Catechist: God is love, and we who abide in love abide in God. We begin this day (or this class) in the presence of the God who is love.
>
> In the name of the Father, and of the Son, and of the Holy Spirit.

Response:	Amen.
Catechist:	May the light of God's love be in us.
Response:	May the light of God's love be in us.
Catechist:	Let us pray. Loving God, you give us St. Valentine as a model of love for each other. As we gather to celebrate the feast of this caring saint, let this candle remind us of your burning love for each of us.

Light the candle.

	May it also inspire us to love others as you have loved us. We ask this through Christ our Lord, who lives and reigns with you and the Holy Spirit, one God forever and ever.
Response:	Amen.

The lector hands his or her box or bag to the catechist, then goes to the bible, bows, and reads 1 John 4:7-12.

Lector:	A reading from the first letter of John. My dear friends, we must love each other. Love comes from God, and when we love each other, it shows that we have been given new life. We are now God's children, and we know him. God is love and anyone who doesn't love others has never known him. God showed his love for us when he sent his only Son into the world to give us life. Dear friends, since God loved us this much, we must love each other. No one has ever seen God. But if we love each other, God lives in us, and his love is truly in our hearts. The word of the Lord.
Response:	Thanks be to God.
Catechist:	I can see the anticipation in your eyes as you wait to receive your gifts. This is the same joy reflected in God's eyes when we care for one another. As we heard in the scripture reading, God loves us deeply and calls us to

love one another. St. Valentine followed that command so faithfully that he has become a symbol of love for all of us.

These cards and treats are signs of our love and care for each other. I invite you now to hold the bags and boxes up for a blessing.

Catechist: Generous God, you love us like a mother and father. You teach us right from wrong, you forgive us when we are sorry for our sins, and you will never leave us. Bless these cards and treats, the signs of our love for one another. In the spirit of your holy bishop, St. Valentine, may these small gifts bring joy and light both to those who give them and to those who receive them. We ask this in the name of Jesus our Lord.

Response: Amen.

Catechist: We will now begin on this side of the circle. I will invite you to go to the people whose names are on the boxes (or bags) that you hold. Wish them a Happy St. Valentine's Day and give them their boxes (or bags). Do not open them yet. After all of you have yours, we will bless ourselves with the Sign of the Cross, and then you may go to your desk to open them.

Name two or three children at a time to present the boxes and bags to each other. There will likely be giggling and laughing, as well as several attempts to open the contents. Simply remind the children that they will open their packages after all have theirs. Allow the giggling unless it becomes disruptive, in which case you may need to request quiet.

Catechist: As we prepare to go to our seats and open our gifts, we bless ourselves once more in the God who is love.

In the name of the Father, and of the Son, and of the Holy Spirit.

Response: Amen.

Catechist: You may now go to your desks to enjoy the gifts we share with each other.

St. Patrick's Day

St. Patrick was born around 385 in Scotland. When he was fourteen, he was taken to Ireland as a slave to herd sheep. He remained faithful to God, even though the people around him were pagan. Patrick escaped when he was twenty and went back to his family in Britain. He was ordained a priest and then a bishop before his dream to take the gospel to Ireland was fulfilled. Patrick worked in Ireland for forty years, preaching, building churches, and converting thousands of people. He died there in 461. The shamrock is associated with Patrick, because he used its three leaves coming from one stem to illustrate the Trinity. Because of his work in Ireland, Patrick has become the patron saint of all things Irish.

Before St. Patrick's Day, have the children cut out green shamrocks.

On the morning of St. Patrick's Day, place the shamrocks on the table around the candle and have a box of pins nearby.

If possible, make some green punch for the children to enjoy at the end of the ritual. To avoid sugar and minimize expense, simply add green food color to ice water.

Process to or simply gather around the candle table.

Catechist: We begin this day (or this class) in the presence of the God who calls us to proclaim the good news to all people.

In the name of the Father, and of the Son, and of the Holy Spirit.

Response: Amen.

Catechist: May the light of God's love be in us.

Response: May the light of God's love be in us.

Catechist: Let us pray. Faithful God, you give us your bishop Patrick as a model of missionary service, as one who dedicated his life to spreading the faith to all who would listen. As we gather to celebrate the feast of this devoted saint, let this candle remind us of your burning love for each of us.

Light the candle.

May it also inspire us to spread the flame of your life and truth. We ask this through Christ our Lord, who lives and reigns with you and the Holy Spirit, one God forever and ever.

Response: Amen.

Catechist: St. Patrick was a missionary and a gifted teacher. He used the shamrock, a native plant in Ireland, to explain the Trinity to the people. He told them that just as the shamrock has three distinct leaves yet is all one plant on one stem, the Father, Son, and Holy Spirit are separate and yet are all one God. Receive this shamrock today as a reminder of your responsibility to share the good news of Christ with your classmates, your families, and your friends.

Pin a shamrock on the shirt of each child. If they are old enough, the students may pin the shamrocks on themselves.

Catechist: Let us pray. Gracious God, you have given us the gift of faith, a gift so wonderful that we want to share it. Help us to live in a way that makes your love shine out to the world.

I invite you now to extend your hands toward each other in the circle for a traditional Irish blessing.

Children extend a hand toward each other.

Catechist: May the road rise to meet you.
May the wind be always at your back.
May the sun shine warm upon your face, the rains fall
     soft upon your fields,
And until we meet again,

May God hold you in the hollow of his hand.
We ask this through Christ our Lord.

Response: Amen.

Catechist: Let us offer each other a sign of peace, and then enjoy a
               cold green drink.

A Saint's Feast Day

This ritual can be used to celebrate the feast day of each child's patron saint. It is best to have a calendar of the feast days in the classroom. At the beginning of the year, circle the feast days of the children in the class and tell them you will incorporate a special celebration for their saints in the lighting of the class candle that day. Before the actual feasts, the children do some research into the biography and special charisms of their patron saints. The catechist then incorporates these charisms into the prayers and invocations of the ritual. If the children can adequately do so, they tell the story of their patron saints in the ritual.

Because of the tremendous diversity in the lives of saints, this ritual is very open-ended and flexible. Feel free to experiment, modifying the ritual as it seems appropriate for a particular saint.

If possible, have a picture, icon, or symbol of the saint on the candle table. A clear bowl of water is also placed on the candle table.

Process to the candle table or simply gather around it.

Catechist:	We begin this day (or this class) in the presence of the God who calls us all to be holy.
	In the name of the Father, and of the Son, and of the Holy Spirit.
Response:	Amen.
Catechist:	May the light of God's love be in us.
Response:	May the light of God's love be in us.

Catechist:	Let us pray. Faithful God, you give is Saint [Name] as a model, as one whose dedication spread the good news and witnessed to your faithful love. As we gather to celebrate the feast of Saint [Name] let this candle remind us of your burning love for each of us.

Light the candle.

	May it also inspire us to spread the flame of your life and truth. We ask this through Christ our Lord, one who lives and reigns with you and the Holy Spirit, one God forever and ever.
Response:	Amen.
Catechist or Student who researched the saint:	Saint [Name] was (tell the story of the saint's life. Include any difficulties the saint faced in following the call of faith. Name any special characteristics, gifts, or charisms that defined this saint).
Catechist:	Let us pray. Gracious God, you have given us this gift of faith, a gift so wonderful that we want to share it. Help us to live in the spirit of Saint [Name] by (give an example of how the saint's life or faith could be lived out by the students).

Call forward the student whose feast is being celebrated. Dip your hand into the water and as you make the Sign of the Cross on the students forehead speak the following:

Catechist:	We ask special blessing today for [child's name].
	He/She has blessed this class and we are grateful for his/her uniqueness. Grant that he/she may know his/her gifts and help him/her to use those gifts for your glory and the good of all your people.
	We ask this in Jesus' name.
Response:	Amen.

Dip your hand again into the water, and as you sprinkle the water over the entire class, repeat the following:

Catechist:	God of life, just as you called Saint [Name], so you call us into holiness. You include us all in the communion of the saints and you long to be near to our hearts. Draw us ever closer to the warmth of your life, the hope of our faith, and the light of your Spirit. We ask this through Christ our Lord, who lives and reigns with you and the Holy Spirit, one God forever and ever.
Response:	Amen.
Catechist:	May God bless our hearts and minds as we learn.
Response:	In the name of the Father, and of the Son, and of the Holy Spirit. Amen.

For a Child Who Is Moving Away

This ritual is written for the end of the last class in which the child who is moving will participate. It can be modified for use during an earlier class.

Before the ritual, encourage members of the class to make goodbye cards telling the child one thing they will miss about him or her and wishing God's blessings. You may want to have a bag or small box in which the child can carry the cards after the ritual.

Pour a little perfumed oil into a small bowl placed next to the lit class candle.

Rehearse with the children the blessing song to the tune of Oscar Mayer Wiener.

The ritual is written with the catechist naming the invocations of the blessing prayer. These may instead be named by various students in the class. Make sure they practice briefly ahead of time so they know when to read their invocations.

When you are ready for the ritual, gather the class around the candle table with the children holding their cards. The child who is moving stands next to the catechist.

Catechist:	This is a time of transition, and all transitions carry with them mixed emotions. We have to leave something behind in order to go on to something new, and even when the change is good, we grieve what we are losing.
	[Name] is moving away and will no longer be a part of our class. We are sad because we will miss her/him. Yet this move brings new opportunities for [name], living in a new place, making new friends, and having new adventures.

As we say goodbye today, we remember with joy the times we have had together. Distance can never take away the memories we have. No matter how far away we are, no matter what happens in the future, we will always be a part of each other.

And so [name] we send you off with blessings in the name of Jesus.

Catechist asks all children to place a hand on the child or, if there are too many children to do so, ask them to raise their hands in blessing. Then lead the class in a litany.

Catechist:	[Name], we thank God for your life.
Response:	We bless you in the name of Jesus.
Catechist:	We thank God for your smile.
Response:	We bless you in the name of Jesus.
Catechist:	We thank God for all the gifts your presence has brought to our classroom. (Add any characteristics the child has exhibited in the class.)
Response:	We bless you in the name of Jesus.
Catechist:	We thank God for the chance to know you, and for the memories we will always treasure.
Response:	We bless you in the name of Jesus.
Catechist:	We ask God to be with you always, and to keep you healthy and strong.
Response:	We bless you in the name of Jesus.
Catechist:	We pray that you will know Jesus better every day.
Response:	We bless you in the name of Jesus.
Catechist:	We pray that you will learn and grow as you and your family face new adventures.

Response: We bless you in the name of Jesus.

Catechist: We surrender you into God's care as we anoint you with
             oil. May it soothe your sadness at leaving and remind
             you that God's Spirit will accompany you in your new
             life to come.

*Dip your fingers in the oil and make the Sign of the Cross on the child's hands. Then
hold the child's hands in yours as you continue the blessing.*

Catechist: God of all creation, you have given us the gift of [name].
             We thank you for the time she/he has been with us, and
             we ask that you keep us always in each other's memory.
             We ask your continued blessings upon her/him and
             her/his family as they enter a new stage of their lives.
             Bless them and keep them, let the fire of your Spirit burn
             ever brightly within them, and grant them peace and
             love wherever they go. We ask this through Jesus Christ
             our Lord, who lives and reigns with you and the Holy
             Spirit, one God forever and ever.

Response: Amen.

Catechist: Your classmates have made cards for you. We give these
             to you now. May they bring a smile when you read
             them, and help you remember the good times we have
             shared together.

*The children give their cards to the child who is moving. They may be placed directly
into the bag or box.*

Catechist: Finally, we sing you our blessing song.

All: *Sing to the tune of the Oscar Mayer Wiener song:*

             May the blessing of the Lord be upon you.
             We bless you in the name of the Lord.
             May the blessing of the Lord be upon you.
             We bless you in the name of the Lord.

Catechist: May Almighty God bless all of us, in the name of the Father, and of the Son, and of the Holy Spirit.

All: Amen.

Optional: Invite the children to give a hug to the one who is leaving.

Published Resources for Other Rituals, Prayers, and Information

Book of Blessings. Collegeville, MN: The Liturgical Press, 1988.

Chateau, Kathy and Paula Miller, *Celebrating Catholic Rites and Rituals in Religion Class.* Mystic, CT: Twenty-Third Publications, 1998.

Haas, David and Robert Piercy, *Walking by Faith.* Chicago: GIA Publications, 1999. Available alone or with accompanying CD.

Halmo, Joan, *Celebrating the Church Year With Young Children.* Collegeville, MN: The Liturgical Press, 1988.

Hynes, Mary Ellen, *Companion to the Calendar.* Chicago: Liturgy Training Publications, 1993.

Jeep, Elizabeth, *Children's Daily Prayer.* Chicago: Liturgy Training Publications, 1999.

Pottebaum, Gerard A., *The Rites of People.* Washington, D.C.: The Pastoral Press, 1992.

Simons, Thomas G., *Blessings for God's People.* Notre Dame, IN: Ave Maria Press, 1995.

Williams, Vivian, *Classroom Prayer Basics.* Laurel, MD: The Pastoral Press, 1997.